AW WITH WORDS

Young Writers' 16th Annual Poetry Competition

It is feeling and force of imagination that make us eloquent.

How can I not dream while writing? The blank page gives a right to dream.

YoungWriters

South West England
Edited by Donna Samworth

 Young**Writers**

First published in Great Britain in 2007 by:
Young Writers
Remus House
Coltsfoot Drive
Peterborough
PE2 9JX
Telephone: 01733 890066
Website: www.youngwriters.co.uk

SB ISBN 978-1 84602 872 4

Foreword

This year, the Young Writers' *Away With Words* competition proudly presents a showcase of the best poetic talent selected from thousands of up-and-coming writers nationwide.

Young Writers was established in 1991 to promote the reading and writing of poetry within schools and to the young of today. Our books nurture and inspire confidence in the ability of young writers and provide a snapshot of poems written in schools and at home by budding poets of the future.

The thought, effort, imagination and hard work put into each poem impressed us all and the task of selecting poems was a difficult but nevertheless enjoyable experience.

We hope you are as pleased as we are with the final selection and that you and your family continue to be entertained with *Away With Words South West England* for many years to come.

Contents

Tamsin Hichens (11) 18
Emily Kerr (11) 18
Daniel Lugg (11) 19
Greg Rowe (11) 19
Matthew Mansell (12) 20
Alexander Nixon (12) 20
Mark Williams (11) 20
Stacy Taylor (11) 21
Jess Price (11) 21
Tegen Williams (11) 22

Colston's Girls' School, Bristol
Rachel O'Donovan (11) 22
Mattie Ward (12) 23
Danielle Bailey (11) 23
Charlotte Fletcher (12) 24
Megan Lawrence (11) 25
Chloe Campbell (11) 26
Katie Smith (11) 26
Reema Mobeireek (10) 27
Lizzy Clarke (13) 27
Mandeep Kaur (12) 28
Tamara Harvey (11) 28
Ellie Edwards (13) 29
Florence King (12) 29
Charlotte Lacey (11) 30
Katie Ahmadi (12) 31
Chanchalraj Kaur (12) 32
Morag Haddow (13) 32
Holly Kilpatrick (13) 33
Lizzie Walker (12) 33
Amelia Zadarnowski (12) 34
Sinead McLarty (14) 34
Sophia Malik (13) 35
Shelley Silvester (14) 35
Stephanie Horne (13) 36
Shannen Griffin (13) 36
Corinne Walker (13) 37
Rebecca Bailey (12) 37
Sabilla Hussain (13) 38
Hannah Lister (13) 38

Hollie Farrow (13)	61
Alice Webber (12)	61
Emily Wright (10)	62
Rose Juliet (11)	63
Mariam Olatidoye (11)	64
Lois Linter	64

Oakmead College of Technology, Bournemouth

Nicole Morris (14)	65
Caroline Allen (16)	65
Helen McCann (14)	66
Nicole Taylor (15)	67
Victoria Oliver (16)	68
Jamie Anderson (14)	69
Tanya Brierley (17)	70
Rachel Moore (16)	70
Ben Gartshore (15)	71
Jessica Moulden (14)	71
Charlotte Franklin (14)	72
Mark Dyer (15)	73
Charlotte Sharp (14)	74
Kate Drummond (14)	75
Carrianne Chandler (14)	76
Lauren Ridout (14)	77
Stephanie Teal (14)	78
Matthew Legg (14)	79
Katy I'anson (15)	80
Carl Penny (15)	81
Kurt Redrup (15)	82
David Foord (15)	83
Dean Derbyshire (15)	84
Alistair Cannings (15)	85
Lauren Clark (15)	86
Alex Gibbs (15)	87
Jacob Stone (15)	88
Chloe Lewis (15)	89
Hayley Cuff (14)	90
Robbie Board (15)	91

Torquay Grammar School for Girls, Torquay

Sophia Peutherer (14)	92
Zoe Lumley (13)	92
Savanna Bonstow (11)	93
Josephine Hanrott (11)	93
Charlotte Walmsley (11)	94
Amy Lett (11)	94
Katie Girow (13)	95
Sophia Nikolaou (12)	95
Constance Collier-Qureshy (11)	96
Emily Roberts (12)	96
Lilly Bertram (12)	97
Sophie Parsons (12)	97
Megan Duff (11)	98
Danielle Orrell (11)	98
Emily Melluish (11)	99
Hannah Gill (13)	99
Sukayna Zayer (11)	100
Imogen Uniacke (12)	101
Hollie Dennison (13)	102
Rebecca Polding (14)	102
Abigail Lowe (13)	103
Holly Badger (12)	103
Juliet Wheeler (13)	104
Kate Guppy (13)	105
Keira Mayne (13)	106
Jasmine Hogg (11)	106
Camilla Wakeford (12)	107
Madeleine Whatmore (11)	107
Rachael O'Hanlon (12)	108
Annabel Seymour (14)	109
Emily Heathcote (13)	110
Rose Brennan (15)	110
Hannah Smith (13)	111
Chloe Tomkinson (11)	111
Georgina McLennan (13)	112
Courtney Giles-Buchanan (12)	113
Jennifer Huntington (13)	114
Beth Dyer (13)	115
Emily Harte (12)	116
Amy Woolfenden (12)	117

Wareham Middle School, Wareham

Writhlington School, Writhlington

Louise Bennett (12)	147
Dannielle Pearce (11)	147
Katie Beck (12)	148
Sam Maggs (12)	148
Samuel Hopkins (12)	149
Nubia Abaka (12)	149
Zoe Fear (12)	150
Adam Simmons (12)	150
Katy Jane Larcombe (12)	151
Eleanor Owen (12)	152
George Beechener (11)	153
Kirsty Cotter (11)	154
Jazuela Wall (11)	154
Ellena Doswell (11)	155
Seona Alexander (14)	155
Tania Reason (12)	156
Aaliyah Porter (11)	157
Martha Cooper (14)	158
Joanne Clapp (14)	158
Claire Andrade (14)	159
Billy Say (11)	159
Caroline Rankin (14)	160
Andrew Girvan (14)	160
Lauren Smith (14)	161
Tabitha Eddleston (14)	161
Polly Eddleston (12)	162
Emma Shaw (14)	163
Jacqui Fee (14)	164
Alice Gouldbourne (12)	164
Guy Solomon (14)	165
Natasha Alsop (14)	165
Emma Robertson (14)	166
Helen Vipond (14)	167
Kate Fawcett (14)	168
Bethan Lewis (11)	168
Joe Seymour (12)	169
Rhiannon Batstone (12)	169
Chloe Hilleard (11)	170
Maddie Norton Smith (12)	171

The Poems

Trapped

Ring of a doorbell, smiles arrive
Pattering footsteps there by your side.
Warmth of your family spread through your veins
Feelings impossible to describe.

Forget all worries, drain from your mind
Love as powerful, builds up inside.
Family, nowhere more special to belong
Dreams I long to come true.

Crashing of doors erupt through the house
Shouting, bellowing echo in the walls.
Glances, make for pieces of dirt,
Feelings impossible to describe.

Dreading home, what happens next.
Tension, nerves, everywhere you turn.
Wondering, dreaming, somewhere else
Alone. Trapped. Cold.

Eilish Harmon-Beglan (14)
All Saints CE School, Weymouth

Obscurity

I look into the shining past,
And wonder, as many do, how did it all go so fast?
The door of obscurity looms ever nearer.
The lock that cannot be undone is trapping me.
The realisation of it all is getting clearer;
The public no longer look at me so admirably.
The friends I once had have run away.
How can they treat their loyal companion with such disdain?
They utter such things I'd never imagine them say.
They just look on at my sudden and turbulent fall from fame.
And as I watch the once familiar limelight fade into the distance,
I think to myself, *that's show business.*

Declan Croft (13)
Beaminster School, Beaminster

Slow Sloth

I, the sloth, slowly slumbered,
Past the fruit-growing tree,
I trudged to the cliff edge,
And looked out to sea,
Where did it all go wrong?
Who tried this human scheme?
Why not stay in the water
Where they should have been?
Why not stay as a river trout?
Why not swim all day?
Why not float in the water?
Why not speed in the bay?
What idiot wanted legs to walk?
Who tried to run on land?
Man had ruined the rolling plains,
Stamped and crushed the sand,
Now oil clots the rivers,
Now forests are sparse and few,
Creatures are hunted only for sport,
Man should start anew
Keep them underwater,
Tie them to the reef,
Pin them to the waves,
Humans should have gills,
And ruin the kingdoms there,
Underwater, I don't mind,
But here, right now, I care.

Rogan Murley (12)
Beaminster School, Beaminster

Abandoned

Why has she left me?
Where is she?
I want her,
I want my mum,
Does she want me?
Am I not pretty?

I lay here
In the rubbish,
I lay here
Wondering.

Will I ever see her again?
I love her
Does she love me?
Will she ever come back for me?

I hear cars,
Lots of them,
They scare me,
Where are they?

People.
I hear people,
Shall I cry?
Maybe they'll hear me,
What if they can't?
No, they have got to hear me,
The baby,
The baby with no name.

Rebecca Smith (12)
Beaminster School, Beaminster

My Poem

What was there?
Two worlds appeared at once
I could not be in both at once
I took the hard one, the one I should
A challenging life was to be had
Not THE easy one the most had
In the world there was no breeze
No fun, not even at the fair
No laughter or joy
What was there?
The rough life was there
Not many travelled through
Hard work every second
Hard tasks lay there waiting
Not brown leaves like in the easy world
Who was there?
The man in charge was the cause of this
He was the type you cannot understand
If you're not working the man will spot you
Hell is your pay
You go down there
Many people were sent down to Hell
The few that weren't were up above
Their life ended in the world
Not a good life, a bad one
The type that not many travelled through.

Chloe Aburrow (12)
Beaminster School, Beaminster

Decisions, Decisions

Every day there are choices to be made
Small things like peanut butter, Marmite
People to listen to, orders to be obeyed
Stay calm or rise to a fight.

The auditions for the panto are taking place,
The disco is too,
Another decision to face.
Which one to go to?
I need to decide.
I said I was going to the disco, I lied!

To get a great part
Or to dance and have fun?
To act and sing
Or to catch up on all the goss?

I went on the stage,
They offered me the place!
I read the script page after page,
There wasn't music, not a trace.

But still I had fun,
Not at the disco,
After umming and ahhing
I made the right choice.

Molly Elsworth (12)
Beaminster School, Beaminster

We Were Best Friends Once

I have a best friend, Cressida
We used to do everything together
But then we were split up,
She went one way, I went the other
We were best friends once.

She has new friends and I do too
But I know she still remembers me,
Everyone always hated us
But that never stopped us
We were best friends once.

Then, on a Saturday, three years later,
Guess who I saw walking down the street?
Cressida!
Her new friends are tall and they are cool
We will be best friends forever now.

Evangeline Abbott (12)
Beaminster School, Beaminster

Speechless

As I walk down the road I see people chatting,
Oh I wish I could do so.
Girls fighting over their loved ones, verbal use,
Why do they use it like that?
In shops I see people's mouths moving,
They're wasting their breath.
Would they ever spare a word for me?
I don't think so,
Should I try and say or leave it be?
Nothing comes out,
I think it's just me.

Katie Hunt (12)
Beaminster School, Beaminster

My Poem

Today will just be another day,
Like all the rest, the same.
I know your water is easy to get
Ours isn't,
You can just go to the tap
I have to walk two miles to get it
I know your houses are warm,
Ours isn't,
You can just sit by the radiator and warm up
We have a cold hut with a fire burning
I know you have spare time to play with,
I don't,
You can see friends or go shopping
I have to help fetch wood and carry water
I know you have rain sometimes,
We don't,
You can go and splash about in the puddles
We dance for the rain to come every night
I know you have a varied diet,
We don't,
You have eggs, fruit and vegetables
I have rice, porridge and fish if we're lucky
I know you have friends to see and talk to,
My friends are all ill or unhappy mostly,
You have a happy life,
I don't.

Gemma Smith (13)
Beaminster School, Beaminster

Getting Old

Darkness, darkness, everywhere I turn,
I cannot read and cannot learn.
I used to be the top boy in school,
Following every single rule.
But that was so long ago from today,
As the month twists into early May.
Another year and a story told,
Another of my friends gone now there are only a few of us
And we are getting old.

I remember writing about my adventures and lies,
And how I would always win first prize.
Those school days were the best of my life
But they couldn't last.
I got a job, made a living
But I was always giving -
My life wasted away.
Thinking about it today
I regret what I have not done in my life
Hit by a heavy knife
The grip of tiredness and old age
Like someone turning the final page
We are getting old.

My sight begins to fail me,
So much so I can no longer read.
And the days drift on and on.
The leaves sweep over my friend's grave,
Will that be me tomorrow, the fears and pain?
And we are getting old.

Lucy Hensher (12)
Beaminster School, Beaminster

Fear

It's cold and wet
As I lay on the road.
Hit by two lights,
As it started to snow.
Then two more lights,
Bright, then dark.
Someone stepped out,
Not bothering to park.
The wind blew hard,
Down through the street.
A blanket so warm,
Wrapped around me.
I soon woke up,
Next to a fire.
A pain running through me,
A mixed desire.
A few days pass,
I felt much better.
A rush of cold air,
Brushed through my feathers.
The cage was opened,
As I sat inside.
Two steps forward,
I flew with pride.

Felicity Waller (12)
Beaminster School, Beaminster

Sorrow's Smile

She sat in the aged oak
On a bent branch
Swinging her tired legs
With the weary rhythm
Of loss
She stared at the gleaming red apple
In her pallid palm
She dug her nails in
Letting all her anger
Grief and regret
Pass like a spark
Into the ripe fruit
She withdrew her nails
And hurled it to earth.
It exploded.
Shattering like glass
Into a million pieces
Of rancid fruit,
Just like
Her pitiful life.
Through her thoughtless tears,
She offered the sky
Sorrow's smile.

Kate Bertram (16)
Bryanston School, Bryanston

Hunger

A gripping emptiness,
Forcing your stomach away,
Squeezing and gripping
Steaming it tries to crawl back
Reaching for a plunger, it explodes
Popping and curling it comes back.

Ewan Wallace (11)
Cape Cornwall School, Penzance

My Birthday

It's my birthday today
My friends sing hip hip hooray,
I'm blowing up balloons,
They're going to be here soon.

I want a new bike
To replace my old trike,
There's a knock on the door,
I'm a big *one four!*

I'm buying a new bra,
Soon I'll be in a car,
I was meant to have a cake,
Which my mum forgot to bake.

I've had a great day,
And I'd just like to say,
Hip hip hooray!

Eilidh Armstrong (11)
Cape Cornwall School, Penzance

Happiness Poem

I feel so happy
When I'm out on a ride,
Out on the moors
I'm sitting astride.
As we gallop
And canter about,
I feel so happy
That I shout out!
When it's dreary,
Drip, drip rain,
I go out and fill
A hay net in vain.
Riding is my favourite thing,
Happiness is the best thing!

Morwenna Charman (11)
Cape Cornwall School, Penzance

Loneliness

It feels as if I'm all alone,
It truly feels like you're on your own,
It's like you're blue, you're jammed in two,
You can't describe it in many words,
You have to think of singing birds,
Nobody likes being on their own,
Some people try to moan and moan,
But it's not the way to solve the problem
But someone's got to stop 'em, stop 'em.

Rosie Brenton (11)
Cape Cornwall School, Penzance

Popping Up And Down

Popping up and down, round and round
You're making me dizzy
You can't control yourself
It feels like you're one big bouncy ball
Popping up and down, round and round.
My head is popping with happiness,
I can't hold it in.

Ruby-Mae Williams (12)
Cape Cornwall School, Penzance

Hunger

A fist in your stomach forcing pain into your throat,
Hurting so dearly, forcing a scream, but you can't
Because you're already eating on your own pain.
You see home down a long and cobbled road
The fist crawling toward your heart.
You feel your soul being sucked into oblivions
You fall screaming and losing hope
Gripping onto a pole, pushing your own pain down and out.

Thomas Ashton (12)
Cape Cornwall School, Penzance

Happiness

Galloping, breezing against my face,
Riding with power, changing our pace.
Happiness, joyfulness goes straight to my brain
Then suddenly it begins to rain.
Starting to trot, sunshine appears,
Then jumping off, it begins to get hot,
Lying, gazing, smelling the daisies.
Emptiness erupts inside of me,
Feeling no emotion but having to smile,
While I lie there I hear a whinny
I remember, I begin to grin.

Chelsea Bailey (12)
Cape Cornwall School, Penzance

Jealousy Burns

An explosion comes; you see the golden item,
Glowing in the hand of the irritating girl,
She is squeezing the magic object,
Stroking it, boasting about it to the boy next door,
Popping it, forcing it over the wall so the boy can see it,
My blood boils when I see her give me the evils,
I just want to put a bomb in her knickers. He! He!
Gripping with all her might so she doesn't drop the golden item
Jealousy burns! I need it, I want it! I will have it now!

Dorothy Best (11)
Cape Cornwall School, Penzance

Jealousy

I felt the trees leaning down on me, squeezing my guts out.
'Help, help, help Dad, help, I am falling, falling down the tree, *ouch!*
My back, it's hurting, hurting very much.'
'Are you alright Alice?'
'Yes Dad, yes I am.'

Alice Farnham (11)
Cape Cornwall School, Penzance

Riding Home

I spring into the saddle and hold tight onto the reins;
A fast and furious canter, we ride across the plains.

The leaves begin to tremble as the wind now starts to blow,
The storm is fast approaching and I wish I was at home.

And now I'm riding faster and the wind, it starts to whine.
The angry clouds that scowl at me send shivers down my spine.

The lightning is so bright it turns to day what once was night,
And the thunder crashes overhead and gives me such a fright.

I'm galloping at my fastest now and racing against time,
And I'm thinking to myself, *will I reach home before nine?*

The numbing rain and icy wind battle hard against my face,
I'm glad I had my Weetabix to help me keep this pace.

I round the final corner as the tempest nears its height,
The lantern by the stable door says home is now in sight.

My steed knows it's close now, its heart is pounding fast,
We ride into the courtyard; we're home, safe at last.

Rosanna Ceredig-Evans (12)
Cape Cornwall School, Penzance

Hunger

Your stomach being swirled slowly around,
The nothing inside pushing, crawling its way to the back of your throat,
A special visit from the stomach taker,
Your mind growing with delectable thoughts
Feel yourself getting thinner, lighter,
Feel the stomach pain getting bigger, stronger,
The voice calling, 'Aches,' getting louder, growing,
Desperately making you chew your insides,
Your body and brain jumbling about inside your stomach.

Ellie Brolly (11)
Cape Cornwall School, Penzance

Happiness

A smiley face,
A warm cuddle,
A duvet of warm protecting shields,
A soft furry cat purring
And protecting you from any danger.

The warming sun keeping everything warm
And keeping evil at bay,
A happy face,
A summer day,
A newborn lamb,
A day in May,
Everything alive and happy,
Happiness everywhere.

Jonathan Kirman (11)
Cape Cornwall School, Penzance

Anger

When anger is hot,
It comes like fire.
It came all hot,
When three brats of some boys called my brother a liar.
I beat them up
And burnt their skin
And when they were dead
I danced around them in a big hot ring.

After that
I cooked their skin
And ate it for supper,
Then puked it up in the bin.
After that,
My brother ate their eyeballs
Then told his mates that they were tasty
And cool.

Gemma Willis (11)
Cape Cornwall School, Penzance

Anger

I felt angry, I felt like punching someone,
I could hear a squeaky voice whispering to me,
I wanted to run as fast as I could to get away from my painful anger,
I felt like someone was gripping me tight so I couldn't get away,
Steam was coming out of my ears,
I felt a screaming noise coming behind me,
Then I realised it was me belching my voice out,
I wanted to cry but I was forcing myself not to.

Molly Compton-Cashmore (11)
Cape Cornwall School, Penzance

Jealousy

Boasting voices spinning round my head,
Longing to go and get the item,
Tummy curling into a little ball,
Unfairness popping up inside you,
Stretching you out to see how much you want it,
Gripping tenseness creeping, creeping down your back,
Envying bubbles erupting in your head,
Go on, get it, you know you want to.

Julia Ellis (12)
Cape Cornwall School, Penzance

Hunger

Yum-yum, chips in my tum
Chicken in the bargain barrel
My tum hurts because it's been two hours
The crispy chicken smells so good
I think I'm going to be sick.
It feels like a cold blade twisting inside me, rumbling
The smell haunts me, it hurts!

Rebecca Hall (11)
Cape Cornwall School, Penzance

Happiness

Happiness brings a warm tinkle inside of me
To make my smile stretch into a wide open shape
But no, I can't resist
I have to make it into a ball of laughter
Even though my throat gets sore I still smile like never before
My smile will never stop popping out of me
It's like a rainbow from grains of happiness
About to melt into a tasteful stream of joy.

Zoe Ley (11)
Cape Cornwall School, Penzance

Lonely

As red as it was outside,
I was awake in bed,
I felt so lonely at 3.45
And so lonely in my head.

On that lonely Tuesday
I was so upset,
I had nothing to say on that Tuesday
Then the sun said bye and set.

Elizabeth Jay (12)
Cape Cornwall School, Penzance

Hunger

I was really hungry,
Coming back from a walk,
I looked in the fridge with a knife and fork
I felt my intestine going really torte,
I couldn't help it,
I was getting so bored,
When is dinner?
I thought, I thought.

Steven Mannering (11)
Cape Cornwall School, Penzance

Happiness

Swirling, soaring in my own world,
Bouncing, bobbing, my smile uncurled,
Bright and beautiful colours outside,
As a butterfly flutters and glides.

Joyful, joking as I skip around,
Smiling, singing far away from the ground,
The happy emotion is warm and curvy,
It is sadness gone topsy-turvy.

I feel it as I do things I like,
Riding my horse, riding my bike,
I feel it at the end of the day,
I'm happy now, *hip hip hooray!*

Tamsin Hichens (11)
Cape Cornwall School, Penzance

Loneliness

Hiding in a corner in a little way,
Wanting to stay there all of the day.
Don't know what to do, should I stay or should I go?
Don't know how to do this, wanting to say no.
How should I help myself being lonely all the way?
Down the line to Hell and the rest by the day,
How to be happy but no, I'm sad.
I don't know what to do or how to be glad.
It's just I want to be there in the heat and the warm,
But no, I have to be here, sitting on my own.

Emily Kerr (11)
Cape Cornwall School, Penzance

Loneliness

A cold, dark evening walking home from school
Feeling lonely I hear a noise behind me
Creaky, groaning, whistling,
Feeling scared I look around, but no one is there!
Scared, lonely, feeling like the only person in the world,
I hear the noise again; cold fear grips and crushes me,
Heart thumping, stomach turning, desperate loneliness.
Looking behind I realise it is only the wind, relief floods through me
Feel foolish, it's only the wind I tell myself
But the loneliness will still be there.

Daniel Lugg (11)
Cape Cornwall School, Penzance

Hunger!

Stomach squeezing hammers,
Dull thought,
Food pictures in your mind,
Rumbling stomach,
Something gripping you,
No hope,
Locked up in a cage,
No way out!
Lungs tensing,
Dealing with hunger,
Brain twisting,
Belly bulging,
Rapid blood,
Hunger!

Greg Rowe (11)
Cape Cornwall School, Penzance

Happiness

A fistful of joy like warm gooey honey building up inside you
Steaming with fun, happiness and amazement
While pushing you up to Cloud Nine!
You try to speak, but you can't because everything good
is squeezing you
It is pushing you into where nothing is bad
Forcing you, urging you to Wonderland
When you're really on Earth, having something pleasant
happen to you.

Matthew Mansell (12)
Cape Cornwall School, Penzance

Anger

A feeling forcing to be used,
Gripping your thoughts,
Crawling through our brain
Pushing any other thoughts up and out of your mind
Squeezing you and not letting go
It reaches your whole body
Stretching you to your limits.

Alexander Nixon (12)
Cape Cornwall School, Penzance

Emotions

Anger is a sign of
Nastiness, round and black
Creeping to you, stabbing behind your back,
It doesn't make a sound
Small, round, red, beady eyes
Makes you want to push your door shut
Feels like no one on the Earth
Understands you or knows you
It is called anger, the dreaded feeling.

Mark Williams (11)
Cape Cornwall School, Penzance

Anger

Storming to the bedroom, tears coming to the eyes,
Push the door open and flop onto the bed
Thinking of everything that's happened.
Angrily start looking through drawers looking for a ball
Then, making the way back to bed, starting to squeeze the ball,
Wishing it was someone's head.
Next, there's a bang, the ball explodes, starting to cry even more,
Waiting to eventually fall asleep so the anger will go away.

Stacy Taylor (11)
Cape Cornwall School, Penzance

Sadness

My bones are rattling
Scared and lonely
I don't know what to do
Shaking
I can hear my heart pumping
Bang!
I can hear myself in my head
Frightened and worried
Running away from my own brain
Run, run, *bang, bang!*
I'm really scared now!

Jess Price (11)
Cape Cornwall School, Penzance

Jealousy Vampire

Leaking into your mind,
Seeping in, thoughts of desire gripping you,
The gaping mouth absorbing your consciousness,
Taken by the monster, curling around the peaceful sanctuary
of your mind,
Staring out at the victim through the glass of your eyes,
No escape,
Eyes glow, reminding yourself of what small things you have.

Tegen Williams (11)
Cape Cornwall School, Penzance

Mrs Lange's Class

We came into the new classrooms
That smelt fresh like flowers.
The first week was fun,
All that seemed to happen was laughter.
Then it was harder,
We started lessons
And the smell of the school meals
Wafted in, making us feel sick!

Quickly, the classroom was brightly coloured,
Reds, blacks, blues, greens, golds and purples.
The classroom still smelt of flowery perfume
But the breaktime milk started to go sour.

When it drew towards Easter
We would go to the pond to see all the new life.
As Easter turned over and May came in, so did SATs.
We hated the stress but when they ended it was great,
Parties, presents and treats for one whole month.
Finally, June came and we stepped out into the big world
Like chicks hatching not knowing what to expect!

Rachel O'Donovan (11)
Colston's Girls' School, Bristol

First Day At A New School

The beeping of the lights as you cross the road,
Getting closer and closer to your new school.
Your head buzzes as you try to remember the gate codes.
You enter a big building asking people directions.
Finally, you get to your classroom,
Your teacher comes in and you all stand up.
Later, your head is rattling with too much information,
You feel tired and ready for break.
You go to lunch eager to eat,
Your tummy rumbles and you dig in.
In seconds your plate is wiped clean.
At break, people chat and run around like mad people.
By the end of the day, all you want to do is go to bed.

Mattie Ward (12)
Colston's Girls' School, Bristol

A Day In Year 5

In my classroom
There's a lot of noise,
Especially with all the boys.
My teacher, Miss Furness,
Has already spilt paint down her dress!

Miss Furness is also a good PE teacher,
It was her special feature,
She made us run a field length and back,
Whilst she ate her snack.

She used to blow a whistle,
Until she got stung by a thistle,
Even though she was so funny,
We liked her as much as honey!
(We love honey!)

Danielle Bailey (11)
Colston's Girls' School, Bristol

A Day At My Old School

My heavy eyelids drooped,
Mr Bartlett mumbled on about fractions,
I daydreamed through the boring lesson,
Suddenly awoken by my best friend poking me
Telling me it was my turn.
I walked slowly up to the white board,
Started to fill in the square boxes,
This reminded me of lovely, smooth Dairy Milk Cadbury's chocolate,
My mouth watered as the bell went,
I quickly rushed out of the door.

I entered the big hall and my teacher seated us,
I was next to one of my friends,
Whilst our Head was talking about term stuff,
We started chatting; suddenly the Head started screaming at us,
Like a howler monkey,
We had detention,
We started to moan but we didn't dare talk,
Then we walked out.

It was breaktime,
We walked slowly to the detention room,
We sat near the front as a teacher was writing something down,
Suddenly, I heard a blood-curdling scream,
It came from outside,
I could see my best friend had fallen off the monkey bars,
Two large dinner ladies waddled, as if they were penguins,
                                      to where she lay,
She unsteadily stood up and I felt so sorry for her,
Someone later said she had broken her arm and gone home.
At home time my whole class were outside,
Everyone talked about that day's high points,
We were like a pack of wolves gossiping away!

Charlotte Fletcher (12)
Colston's Girls' School, Bristol

In Ms Snook's Class

When Ms Snook walked into the room
We all stood up as usual
She said, 'Good morning girls,'
In her normal happy tone
And we started English.

She would say to us,
'Keep working this hard
And you will get a treat at the end of the lesson.'
The room was silent,
The only noise was the sound of fountain pens.

Ms Snook would come round to check our work
'Are you getting on OK?'
She carried on round the class.

'Right girls, put down your pens and listen,
As you have worked so hard
It's time for X-Factor.'

We would take it in turns to sing our own songs
Then we would all sing
Including Ms Snook
A song from Grease!

Then the bell would go.
We would all sigh and say, 'Ooh.'
The lesson ended
'Goodbye girls, see you all tomorrow.'
And it all started again.

Megan Lawrence (11)
Colston's Girls' School, Bristol

Miss Wyn

In the morning we would
Dress up as crazy Egyptian ladies
And paint our faces at our own pace
As we were making a mess.
Miss would show her funky dress
The next hour we would be travelling
Down the river that no one could pronounce.

Miss Wyn was a strange lady
Because she wore funny and neat clothes
Like the next page of your notebook.
With brown curly hair
Tied up with a pink hairband
Like a young sixties girl
With her handy hand painting her face with colour.

The room looked like her face
Shiny when happy
Black when whiny
Pink when she lost her Blu-tack
And gold when friends are around.

Chloe Campbell (11)
Colston's Girls' School, Bristol

Mrs Beer's Jungle

The first step into the room,
To collect that all important slip,
Was enough to make any child's imagination run!
The long toy snake,
The stuffed panda,
The sugar paper branches and tissue paper leaves!
With the paper in your hand,
You would slowly edge out,
The jungle scene filling your mind!

Katie Smith (11)
Colston's Girls' School, Bristol

The Butterfly Lion

Because of feeling lonely
I wanted to feel happiness and joy
One day I turned into a happy boy
When a silk of bright light shone into my life
It was the white prince
It was a lion, a white cub he was
With big shining eyes
You think he seemed dangerous
But look how lucky I was
I felt happy that day
Until one day I had to go away
And my lion had to go to a circus
I didn't want him to be under focus
Now I'm older and I'm a soldier
And I found my white prince, but now he's a king
And our friendship will always be the main thing.

Reema Mobeireek (10)
Colston's Girls' School, Bristol

The Burial

His boots, his gloves and his scarf
Some people would sit back and laugh
For them each to be so different
Yet all to be so significant
We lay them down there
In the cold morning air
Down in his grave with me standing right by like a knave
But still it is there and it lingers
The memory of his cold dead fingers
I feel this insatiable guilt
It's not something I can hide with a quilt
I feel it'll be there forever
I shan't forgive myself, never.

Lizzy Clarke (13)
Colston's Girls' School, Bristol

If Life Was Just So Simple

If life was just so simple,
The world would be at peace.

If life was just so simple,
There would be no hatred.

If life was just so simple,
The world would be calm.

If life was just so simple,
Old people wouldn't get wrinkles.

If life was just so simple,
People would get along with each other.

If life was just so simple,
The streets would be clear.

If life was just so simple,
There would be no problems.

But life isn't so simple,
The world will never be at peace.

Mandeep Kaur (12)
Colston's Girls' School, Bristol

Miss Barnett

Miss Barnett was tall, thin and pretty
You could have said she was a good lookin' Britney.
With long blonde hair tied back in a band
You'd think she was a mermaid lying on the sand.
Wearing a long fashionable dress or just jeans and a vest.
Her favourite subjects were music, drama and art
She taught them all, she was awfully smart!

Tamara Harvey (11)
Colston's Girls' School, Bristol

The Bravest Brother Ever

Charlie is my big brother,
He's the bravest brother ever.
He does not cry, he does not weep,
He doesn't, never ever.

Charlie is my protecting brother,
He's the bravest brother ever.
He will hit for me, he will punch for me,
He will forever and ever.

Charlie is my loving brother,
He's the bravest brother ever.
He'll always love me and be kind to me,
He'll be like that forever.

Charlie is my big brother,
He's the bravest brother ever.
He does not cry, he does not weep,
He doesn't, never ever.

Ellie Edwards (13)
Colston's Girls' School, Bristol

The Hairy Hand Of Dartmoor

I drove across the misty moors
And saw a hairy hand,
It grabbed my wheel
And turned me left
Right across the land,
I tried to catch
This hairy hand
This hairy hand I saw,
But then I knew it mustn't have been
A myth anymore.

Florence King (12)
Colston's Girls' School, Bristol

In Mr Smith's Class

You could fight
The Second World War
Hide in a bunker
Under your desk.
Dressed up as evacuees
We ate our rations for lunch,
Singing, 'We'll meet again.'
We marched home.

Mr Smith, so tall and lanky,
Rides a motorbike.
Young and married
To a woman half his size.
Give him a chocolate
And he'll love you,
But make a mess
Beware!

Don't talk if the noise 'o' meter
Says silent
Or you will lose a sticker,
Keep the classroom tidy
And your work will
Go on one of the
Big bright displays.

Band practice on Thursday nights
Lord of the Rings blasting
From woodwind, string and brass.
Harry Potter and The Beatles.
The school CD rocks
And always will.

Charlotte Lacey (11)
Colston's Girls' School, Bristol

The River

The day by the river was peaceful,
We were sat on the grass by the tree,
Then out of the blue,
Charlie stripped and Molly too.

They ran across the grass,
I could hear their feet squish into the mud,
They jumped into the river,
With a splash and loud screams.

They dared me to join them,
No way would I do it.
I sat by the bank sulking and watched them,
I could feel the cold drops from their splashes run down my face.

A few days later,
When the sun was shining brightly,
We went back to the river
They stripped once again and I joined them.

Covering myself as I ran for the river,
I felt the squishy mud on my feet as I ran,
And I jumped at such force
That I bombed the water.

The coldness and the wetness, we splashed and giggled,
Then we raced to get dried and dressed,
The best day ever, just the three of us,
Molly, Charlie and me forever.

Katie Ahmadi (12)
Colston's Girls' School, Bristol

Molly's Illness

Molly is a great girl, so good and kind
And oh yes, she is mighty fine.
With two plaits and a lovely dress
She never looks like a mess.

We did fun things like hunting and swimming
Luckily, we are still living.
But the worst thing happened when she got scarlet fever
When we found out about this we ran to her, more than a metre.
We were not allowed to see her because of her stubborn parents.

We missed her the most
But she recovered and all is well.
We will love her for the rest of her life,
Yes, we shall!

Chanchalraj Kaur (12)
Colston's Girls' School, Bristol

That Day

(Based on 'Private Peaceful' by Michael Morpurgo)

I buried a mouse
And now the house
Has changed for evermore.

My mother is sad
And I am bad,
My father has gone.

The tree was falling,
My father was sawing,
He jumped in front and died.

He saved my life
And now his wife
Is alone for evermore.

Morag Haddow (13)
Colston's Girls' School, Bristol

There's A Monster In My Bedroom

There's a monster in my bedroom,
I'm so sure.
It hides when I am there,
Under the floor.

Its hideous grin, yellow and crooked
Those eyes glare out, scarlet and wicked.
At night when I am tucked up in bed,
His nightmarish roars creep into my head.
They twist and turn, until nothing makes sense,
I pull the covers up, my only defence.
His low footsteps sound, the floorboards creak,
In the pitch-black, I let out a shriek.
Lights beam out, I turn slowly round,
I fear this is the beast I've found.
But there are no red eyes or yellow teeth,
It is only my dad, what a relief!
He picks me up and gives me a hug,
Then wraps me up in bed all snug.

There's no monster in my bedroom,
That's for sure.
But what's that scratchy noise
Under the floor?

Holly Kilpatrick (13)
Colston's Girls' School, Bristol

The Swallow In The Church

I see the swallow swoop up high in and out of the church beams.
The swallow stops, looks down, down at the door.
Big Joe notices and runs to the door and pushes it open.
The swallow is free to do as he pleases, to swoop, to swish, to sing.
I'll never forget that swallow because it was my father.

Lizzie Walker (12)
Colston's Girls' School, Bristol

Helpless

Molly's voice so blissful in my ear
Was not going to be there for a while to hear.
The dark deaths play of scarlet fever echoing more and more
At poor old Molly's door.
A doorway through Hell is where she lives
No freedom, no light, no welcoming stories in the night.
Stuck up in a room all day, dreaming in a bed of illness that
                                                could spread.
No longer do we hear the sound of Molly's footsteps pounding down
We're all alone, once again where we began till the end.

Amelia Zadarnowski (12)
Colston's Girls' School, Bristol

The Meadow

I stroll into a field of green
And lay down in a meadow,
Where grass is bright and minty green
And buttercups bright yellow.
Butterflies they flutter by
All red and pink and white,
And the oak it rustles in the breeze
And lets in dappled light.
And as I look up at the sky
I see some floating sheep,
Puffy, white and innocent
As I'm falling asleep.
And just as I roll over
I look up at blue skies,
I'm calm, relaxed and tired
And so I close my eyes.

Sinead McLarty (14)
Colston's Girls' School, Bristol

Sweets

Sticky toffee, rainbow drops
These are my favourite sweets.
Fruity tootie, jelly beans
And tasty chocolate treats.
Although they rot my teeth out
I'm addicted to their charm
They call me closer, closer
Until all sweets are gone.
There are so many different sweets
Each one has a unique taste.
But liquorice, old, and stale sweets
Have a really nasty taste
I'm sure you all love sweeties
Guess what, I do too!
Because if you have any sweeties
I'm coming after you!

Sophia Malik (13)
Colston's Girls' School, Bristol

The Holidays

I like the holidays,
But oh how they come and go!
Winter's here,
All crisp and clear.
Snowball fights
And Christmas lights.
Sand in your toes,
Then blowing your nose.
Summer's here all out to play
But autumn's back just the next day.

Shelley Silvester (14)
Colston's Girls' School, Bristol

Suicide

Suicide is the easiest way out,
It is without a doubt.

I am the girl who you said was gay,
I am the girl who had a bad day,
You spat on my back,
Put frogs in my sack,
Now I have taken the easiest way out
And it was without a doubt, the easiest way out.

I put the razor to my mouth
And swallowed it whole,
I heard the scream of my mother,
The shout of my dad,
It was without a doubt, the hardest way out.

Stephanie Horne (13)
Colston's Girls' School, Bristol

The Girl

The girl you undermined,
The girl you stared at,
The girl you laughed at,
The girl you made fun of,
The girl you whispered about,
The girl you called ugly,
The girl who felt alone,
The girl who felt unloved,
The girl who harmed herself,
The girl in the corner,
I am that girl.

Shannen Griffin (13)
Colston's Girls' School, Bristol

It

A rich man walked past today
I've seen him walk here before.
I've seen him on posters,
Seen him on windows and doors.

They always come here,
Flashing their money around.
They look down and ask me to move,
Their faces turned down in a frown.

I sigh and say, 'Sorry for living.'
I move on but where do I go?
Where do I go?
Tell me, I need to know.

Taxis drive past,
My money did not last.
Ain't no use in trying,
I've thought about dying.

No one in this town takes any notice
People are so selfish,
They tell me to stop complaining,
But I'd like to see you get through this.

I'd like to see you *try.*

Corinne Walker (13)
Colston's Girls' School, Bristol

The Ghost

He paces along the corridor
A smile upon his face,
He steps into a photo
And disappears without a trace.
For no one in the house knows who he is,
This disappearing man.
A ghost is what they call him
All across the land.

Rebecca Bailey (12)
Colston's Girls' School, Bristol

I Remember . . .

I remember . . .
The bright day,
The sun shining from far away,
The calm sea flowing by,
The rustling trees that made me cry.

I remember . . .
The sudden shock,
The darkness giving me a knock,
The evenings becoming dark,
The thunder leaving its mark.

I remember . . .
The light giving me hope,
How can I cope?
The bright and dreamy stars,
Shooting right across Mars.

I remember . . .

Sabilla Hussain (13)
Colston's Girls' School, Bristol

Birthday Party

It's your birthday, what should we bake?
How about a big chocolate cake?
What party games should we play?
You choose, it's your special day.
What was your favourite gift?
Definitely my Playmobil lift!
Quick, change into your party dress,
This house will be such a mess!
The boy I fancied gave me a wink!
I had to do something . . . so I offered him a drink.
This was the best of all the parties
I ate lots of sweets, mostly Smarties.

Hannah Lister (13)
Colston's Girls' School, Bristol

Last Christmas

Smoke in the air,
Which floats towards
Our brown Christmas tree,
Chips from the takeaway,
This isn't a proper Christmas Day.

Happy on the outside,
Not on the inside,
I have to be brave,
He's coming to get me,
This isn't a proper Christmas Day.

There was tension,
He entered the room,
Hurling abuse,
He came towards me,
And that was my last Christmas Day.

Ayanna Sharp (13)
Colston's Girls' School, Bristol

The Path Of Life

Who am I Mother?
Another meaningless soul?
Oh please tell me Mother
I'm losing control.
Please save me Mother
I'm burning up inside,
Don't leave me on my own Mother
For you do not want me to die.
Where does it end Mother?
From world to world,
It's all the same
The path of life,
But who's to blame
Me?

Antonia Self (13)
Colston's Girls' School, Bristol

Who Am I?

I am someone who can walk,
I am someone who can talk,
I can read,
I can write,
Who am I?

I'm confused,
Sometimes I'm happy,
Sometimes I'm sad,
Sometimes I'm here,
Sometimes I'm there,
Who am I?

What do I look like?
What do I sound like?
I've never been seen,
I've never been heard,
Who am I?

What am I?
Am I human?
Am I animal?
Do I learn?
Do I read?

Can you guess
'Cause I'm totally confused!

Charlotte Longhurst (13)
Colston's Girls' School, Bristol

Nag, Nag, Nag

'Do your homework,
Clean your room!
Walk the dog,
Shut the door!
Don't forget this,
Don't forget that.'
Nag, nag, nag!

'Shine your shoes,
Get dressed!
Go to bed,
Don't eat it!
It's not teatime yet,
Eat your veg.'
Nag, nag, nag!

'Clear the kitchen,
Get off the computer!
Share that with your sister,
Put a jumper on!
You're not going out like that,
Clean out the guinea pigs.'
Nag, nag, nag!

I can't take anymore!

Alex Gummer (12)
Colston's Girls' School, Bristol

One Day

Not now but one day, will I love you so?
Not now but one day, will I let you go?

Not now but one day, shall this life not end?
Not now but one day, will I take you as a friend?

Not now but one day, will I keep you near?
Not now but one day, will I leave you dear?

Not now but one day, had I thought so hard.
Not now but one day, we wouldn't be apart.

Not now but one day, shall you forget?
Not now but one day, was the day we met.

Not now but one day, if our love was true.
Not now but one day, I would be with you.

Not now but one day, in this lifetime,
Not now but one day, I would be with you.

Khushboo Chandiramani (13)
Colston's Girls' School, Bristol

I Love Christmas

I feel the cold breeze
We cuddle in blankets
To feel the warmth
I love Christmas.

Drinking hot chocolate
With marshmallows,
Presents and fun
Happiness and love.

This is an event
That everybody adores,
All the family gathers around the fire,
I love Christmas.

Saraphina Finch (12)
Colston's Girls' School, Bristol

My Grandmother

I sat by her side
I held her hand
I heard her
Rasp and gasp for breath
My grandmother.

I watched by her bed
I spoke to her
I talked of unimportant things
Chatter - didn't matter right then
My grandmother.

I saw her petal-thin face decay
Wither right away
A delicate flower
Pale and frail forever
My grandmother.

I sat at her grave
I watched at her funeral
I saw her face
I'd swear she was there but . . . I'll miss her
My grandmother.

Elske Waite (13)
Colston's Girls' School, Bristol

Autumn

The wind gushing
Roughly through the plants.
Leaves falling from the trees
Like fairies they slowly drift.
In all colours red and gold
Like a fire burning bright.
Slowly touching the icy cold ground
And there they lie.
Leaving the trees to be forgotten skeletons
Awaiting next summer.

Alice Forty (11)
Colston's Girls' School, Bristol

The Dead Earth

Wasting paper,
Using oil,
Drinking water,
Burning wood.

Stop and think
About what you're doing,
Concentrate,
The Earth is dying.
It's gone
Too late
I told you to stop
But did you listen, *no!*
Now we're paying
By dying here and now!

Joanna Goldsack (12)
Colston's Girls' School, Bristol

We Will Come

We come only by night
Everyone out of sight
We come at full moon
We'll be with you very soon.

We will be knocking at your door
We will be creeping on your floor
We will be searching for your soul
In our cloaks as black as coal.

Soon you'll be with us by our side
Searching for souls because yours has died
We will go out of sight
Until the next fortnight.

Billie Williams (13)
Colston's Girls' School, Bristol

War

Bombs are falling
Children are dying
And there we stand
 Hand in hand
Fighting to save our country.

We go around and see poverty
We see humility
But there we stand
With a rifle in hand
Waiting to kill the enemy.

Why do we fight?
It's a terrible sight
But there we stand
With our lives in our hands
Dying to save our country.

Ocean Pearl Murphy (12)
Colston's Girls' School, Bristol

Wintertime

I watch the snow
Trickle down the window
Slurping my soup
And my cranberry juice.

I step outside
With my coat so wide
And feel the cold bite
I get a shock and a fright.

Back in I go
I've had enough of this snow
Cuddle up in my dressing gown
And under my duvet, down, down, down.

Heidi Brown (12)
Colston's Girls' School, Bristol

Life

Life is such a special thing
Don't let it go away
All these murders and suicides
They're not needed in this day.

Life is such a wonderful thing
Don't let it go away
All this war and hatred
Are not needed in this day.

Life is such a beautiful thing
Don't let it go away
But pollution's taking over
And it's not needed in this day.

But as life is such a brilliant thing
We can turn this world around
If we all work together
A better life can be found.

Ellie Lawrence (12)
Colston's Girls' School, Bristol

Candy

Candy is so luscious
It's sweet, it's sour
It's big, it's small
It's powerful, it's weak
Bonbons are sweet
Yet lemon sherbet is sour
Jaw breakers are big
Whilst Tic-Tacs are small
Willy Wonker's bubblegum is powerful
Mini Milk lollies are weak
Candy can be everything!

Kaydene Lee (11)
Colston's Girls' School, Bristol

Craving

I miss my old friend and need him now more than ever,
So in search of him I sprint down to the newsagents.
As I approach the counter I see him dressed in his persuasive clothes.
My friend is smiling at me as if he has waited his whole life
                                        for this moment,
I pay quickly, not wasting a second.
Ripping off his wrapper in search of the true identity of this
                                        heavenly treat.
I am delighted to make his acquaintance again,
The first mouthful is as good as the last,
It comforts me like a warming hug from my mum.
My heart is pounding as it smiles at me some more,
I am eternally grateful to Mr Cocoa, Mr Milk and Mr Sugar
                                who gave their lives for

Chocolate!

Emma Hennessey (11)
Colston's Girls' School, Bristol

Mute

I watch the world through sealed lips
While people argue, while people bitch
People who can use their tongues
Use them to do harsh wrongs
If I could talk I wouldn't do
All mean things speaking people do
They use their gift to twist and trick
Watching them it makes me sick
But saying that is negative
And I like to be positive
So all in all I do conclude
People are not always rude
And if I forever and ever complain
I am being just the same
So I will not judge, I will not moan
'Cause the seeds of friendship are forever sewn.

Gillian Browne (13)
Colston's Girls' School, Bristol

The Girl Behind The Sun

I see nothing, no one,
I hear them shout and scream,
I call out to them, but nobody comes,
Nobody comes behind the sun.

They try to be kind,
They touch me, they laugh,
But they never come.
Nobody comes behind the sun.

I know what is happening,
But it's in another world.
The day I left they never followed,
Nobody comes behind the sun.

The suffering, the death, the war.
Things which were there, but aren't anymore.
But nothing can touch me, nothing will come
Nobody comes behind the sun.

Savannah Sevenzo (13)
Colston's Girls' School, Bristol

The War

His head full of fright
As he prepares for his fight.
His heart beats so fast
How long will the battle last?
His nose smells the fear
As he sees the enemy near.
His mind thinks of home
His bed soft and warm.
He wants to run and run
To throw away his gun.
He wants the war to end
Change enemy to friend
Say goodbye to his fight
And go home tonight.

Martha Northcott (11)
Colston's Girls' School, Bristol

Daddy's Day

It was Daddy's day today
And she couldn't wait to go.
There were a line of dads against the wall
They all piled into the hall
The teacher began to call out names
To introduce their dads
At last it was her turn
They all turned and stared
And one said, 'Her daddy's not there!'
She didn't care
She went up and said, 'My daddy couldn't make his very special day
He used to be a pilot, a very important man
But one day something happened
Some people took over his plane
And drove into two beautiful buildings
That's why my daddy couldn't make this very special day.'
She told them she didn't miss him
Because when she closed her eyes she could see him.
Everyone started to close their eyes
And to their surprise, it was as if they could see him on one side of her.
Heaven was not too far for him to come on this very special day.

Imogen Livings (11)
Colston's Girls' School, Bristol

Peace

I was in peace from the cool breeze
I was meditating on the Himalayas
I was higher than the sharp rocks
I was cross-legged and my hands were in a figure of peace
The sense of candles filled my nose up
The cool air from the snow made my eyes fresh
The waterway down low filled my mouth with lemon breath
The clouds made my body fill with comfort as the softness touched
Then the sun came into my eyes making me feel like hot fire
                                    and my peace was over.

Annupa Ghedia (12)
Colston's Girls' School, Bristol

Butterfly

Flying by me like an aeroplane
Landing on a pretty rose
Sucking up the pollen
That's a butterfly.

Its wings are so colourful
Like a rainbow in the sky
Bright and beautiful
That's a butterfly.

She flies to her home
Like a bee to a honeycomb
Meeting her family
That's a butterfly.

There she is on a different flower
Collecting her child on the way,
Just like me, caring for others
That's what I am . . . a butterfly!

Hannah Cullum (11)
Colston's Girls' School, Bristol

Photo Day

Photo day hurts my eyes
As the flash shivers down my thighs.
My eyes come out bloodshot-red,
It looks like I've woken from the dead.
I go in all smart, with my collar neatly back,
I come out looking awfully slack.
My hair is tied now, it's a big mess
My blazer was neatly ironed, now it's hardly pressed.
My shoes were jet-black, now they're scuffed and grey
I wonder what I'll look like at the end of the day?

Zara Malik (11)
Colston's Girls' School, Bristol

It's A Nightmare

It's one of those nights again,
Where you feel that fright again,
In the middle of the night again,
When your chest goes tight again,
It's a nightmare.

It's that shape again,
So you go ape again,
It's wearing a cape again,
The hairs on your nape are static again,
It's a nightmare!

Those yellow eyes gleam again,
So your head boils with steam again,
You know what you've seen again,
And it's time to scream again,
It's a nightmare!

Sadie-Mae Churchley (12)
Colston's Girls' School, Bristol

Peace

Peace is like a dove flying over mountains
Whenever it sees a war it tweets a little song
Everybody declares truce and shakes hands.

It flies over villages and stops children fighting
Gives pecks of affection to the good ones
Then flies off again, to help others.

It soars over the hustle and bustle of cities
Lands on the car of a swearing lady
She immediately stops and says sorry.

Peace comes in lots of forms
A dove with a twig in its mouth
Two fingers or the hippy way.

Peace, how lovely!

Charlotte Low (11)
Colston's Girls' School, Bristol

Hope

Hope is a happy word
We use it a lot,
And Hope has a meaning
That should not be forgot.

How is it that Hope can leave us
Just when we need it most?
How can it leave us trembling in the dark
Afraid of some imaginary ghost.

But the truth is Hope is always there
Dancing in the midday sun
And Hope still goes on dancing
Even when day is done.

It's Hope that we all hold on to
Hope that we all cuddle tight,
And hope that those scary monsters
Won't come and scare us again this night.

Becky Holloway (12)
Colston's Girls' School, Bristol

Frustration

Frustration crawls up my spine
When I go to march down to the back of the line.
Frustration sprints towards me
When we're in a rush and Mum decides to get a cup of tea.
Frustration slithers into my thoughts
When I already know something we're trying to get taught.
Frustration runs through my veins
When I just can't get the lion inside me tame.
Frustration sets off a flare
Just like I'm in a nightmare.

Lizzy Clarke (12)
Colston's Girls' School, Bristol

Fear

I see her walk up the stairs
She looks at me stops and glares
I feel her power in my vein
I feel my head throb in pain.

I see her glide towards my door
She glides like a ghost in human form
She glides towards me and touches my head
It gives another throb, I go to bed.

I can't get to sleep
Is she still in my room?
She sits down on my bed
I hear her voice of doom.

She hovers towards my door
And glares at me once more
I hear her slither down the stairs
I can't stand her anymore!

Martha Wood (11)
Colston's Girls' School, Bristol

Fear

Fear creeps up on me
Screams in my ear,
Charges through my body with a giant spear.
He whizzes round the corner and right up to my brain
Everything has frozen; my body's turned to ice.
I start to feel all sticky, sweat pours down my face
Then I realise he's visited me before
And I find myself crouching silently on the floor.

Sophia Doughty (11)
Colston's Girls' School, Bristol

Love

Love is ahhhhh.
Love is ohhhh.
Love strokes and tickles you.
Love is a wink, a smile, a giggle.
Love is a jumper knitted by Nanny Wiggle.
Love is a walk on the beach when the sea
Is a blanket of silk, as white as milk.
It comes and drags you into its cuddly depths.
Love is a chocolate bar sprinkled with sugar.
Love is a puppy, its fur as soft as a feather.
Love is so sweet I've got cavities.
Love is a Galaxy bar, all smooth and luscious.
Love is a munchy, crunchy, chewy, gooey,
Absolutely sensational thing.
Why don't you try it?

Olivia McLeary-O'Neill (11)
Colston's Girls' School, Bristol

The Hottest Season

The snow starts to melt
And the sun peeks out from dark clouds
Like it hasn't come out for years
These are the signs that summer is here.

Dead flowers start to grow into colourful ones,
Your fans are on twenty-four-seven,
Just going out in the scorching heat
Makes you feel like you're on fire.

Drinking a glass of cold ice water
Feels like you are swimming in an ice cream sundae
Going through the mint sauce
While eating chocolate sprinkles.

Angelee Ghedia (12)
Colston's Girls' School, Bristol

What Is A Poem?

A poem is a poem
On a piece of page
It might contain lots of rhymes
That could put you in a rage.

Lines, lines, lines
Words, more words
You have to agree
It's quite absurd.

Words, words, words
Lines, more lines
Stretching on forever
You might run out of time.

Sometimes they're boring
You'd burn them if you could
But it doesn't really matter
As long as they're good.

Beth Norman (13)
Colston's Girls' School, Bristol

Fluff Ball My Cat

She was just like a fluff ball the day she arrived
Unlike the runt of the litter I'm glad she's survived!
Curled in the corner licking her tail
Frightened by the letter box, but it was only the mail!
She spotted in the corner a little white mouse
Off with you, she thought, this is my house!
A few years on she's as plump as can be
But no matter what, she's Fluff Ball to me!

Emily Hurse (13)
Colston's Girls' School, Bristol

Lemonade

Bubbles here and bubbles there,
Bubbles up your nose.
Lemonade should flow down your throat
But that's not the only place it goes.

It makes you hiccup,
It makes you burp,
It always ends up down your skirt.

Drink it at your picnic,
Drink it in the park,
It's guaranteed to make you laugh.

Because there's sugar,
Lemons and additives too,
It has to be the best drink ever,
For both your friends and you.

I love lemonade,
I'm sure that you do also,
I hope that this poem about the wonderful drink,
Makes you love it even more so!

Laura Sinclair (13)
Colston's Girls' School, Bristol

Go For What You Believe In

Go for what you believe in,
Go, go.
No one can stop you from getting to your goal.
You might want to be a doctor,
You might want to be a technician,
But still, at the end, it is a competition.
A competition between you and the time
To work hard, so go for it until you get a sign.
A sign that tells you, you're finally there.
But after you get what you wanted,
Would you still care?

Lina Mobeireek (14)
Colston's Girls' School, Bristol

Mrs Handley's Class

What a start to the day . . . morning assembly, yawn.
No games, no fun, you start to drift away, *bang!*
The bell jolts you awake like your mother's shouting in the morning.
The day is now full of colours, colours of excitement,
Bounciness popping up as you head for her room.
You gracefully pace on, nearer, nearer,
You see the door, you've reached the door, she's gone
It's not the same without her.
The distant bell sounds like a solemn church bell at a funeral.
You trudge down the corridor, heart slowly and painfully sinking,
For your next lesson without her, Mrs Handley.

Alice Stockwell (11)
Colston's Girls' School, Bristol

Where Am I?

The noises are deafening to my ears
Like letting out energy they'd caged up for years.
Smells of all kinds are wafting around
Sniffing harder means new ones are found.
Objects scurrying from here to there
Hustling and bustling with no trace of care.
Everything moving from what I can see
Everything has its purpose, never mind about me.
The only touch is something brushing past
Everything is in a rush, like set to mega fast.
If I sit down I watch them all go by
If I said it wasn't busy that would be a lie.
Everywhere is full of activity
Where am I? I'm in a city.

Zoe Laing (13)
Colston's Girls' School, Bristol

Our Beautiful World

Our world is so beautiful when you look close.
Nature and animals, wild and free,
People who care for you and for me.
Every day we welcome someone new,
But every day we say goodbye too.
Beautiful land, plants and trees,
The summer sun and buzzing bees.
We welcome new life in spring,
We're merry, we dance and sing.
In summer we're hot and wild,
Then comes autumn with weather that's mild.
Winter's my favourite with frost and snow,
Snowflakes that tinkle when temperature's low.
In our world are wonderful animals, it is true,
Cats and dogs and budgies too.
Dolphins that leap as high as the sky,
Eagles and parrots and swans that fly.
But one day soon all this life will die,
Our beautiful world will be gone,
But why?

Stephanie Hare (13)
Colston's Girls' School, Bristol

Ghosts Of 9/11

We are the ghosts of 9/11
We are the men who roared
We are the women who cried
We are the children in Heaven
We should always be remembered
We should always be recalled
We should always be recognised
As the victims of 9/11.

Ejiro Tom-Ezewu (13)
Colston's Girls' School, Bristol

My Primary School

Start of the day was registration
Then on Mondays and Fridays; assembly.
We would do two subjects then break and normally numeracy.
Lunch would come after,
Then some more subjects like science where we would do predictions.

School trips were up to Magotsfield and back.
Once we went to Dean Fields in the Forest of Dean.
We also went swimming, that was really fun!

We sometimes on Fridays would do class assemblies
About things that we had learnt about, like history
(They were always the best in assembly)

Then at the end of the year in Year 6
You would get your school T-shirts signed,
The bell would go at twenty-five past three and you would run
out of the gates
Looking forward to the summer hols and secondary school!

Bethan Hutton (12)
Colston's Girls' School, Bristol

Wolf Woman

Wolf Woman just does not like me
We watch her as she pours her tea.
Before we know it she smells us out
With that long nose which is a snout.
Big Joe is our brother's name
Collecting animals is his game.
But Wolf Woman is so lame
She won't let him keep his same game.
To keep us going, our mother's eyes
Glisten when she leaves us behind,
Wolf Woman, Wolf Woman.

Daisy Scott (12)
Colston's Girls' School, Bristol

Old Schooldays

Looking back I begin to feel small,
From being the biggest and brainiest,
To the smallest, knowing nothing at all.

From red jumpers and white polo shirts,
To navy blue blazers and crisp white blouses,
From navy blue trousers to navy blue skirts.

Four subjects to nine is one big shake,
More books to carry with you all day long,
Making your shoulders feel like they're going to break.

Remembering back to the very first day,
I stepped through the gate,
And I saw my old friend and went to play.

They say time flies when you're having fun,
Well, it definitely took its meaning,
And pop, crack, whizz, the day was done.

Compare it to walking up thousands of stairs,
Going swimming and sports, it all seems so easy,
And getting up early, there is no compare.

But I suppose I'll go on living my life,
Taking one day at a time, waiting for tomorrow,
But I'm sure I can handle the pain and the strife.

Laura Price (11)
Colston's Girls' School, Bristol

Ms Snook

Ms Snook is lots of fun
She's very nice to everyone.
Sometimes she would let us play
But X-Factor happened every day
She said she loved to hear us sing,
But we had to stop when the bell went ding-ding!

Megan Steven (11)
Colston's Girls' School, Bristol

I Loved That Day!

I loved that day!
The way we laughed,
The way we splashed,
I loved that day!

We felt so free,
Giggling and splashing,
Having such a good time,
Together forever, just us three.

The frostbites gave me tickles in my feet,
My hands were tingling like mad
Charlie's face was plum-purple,
But still Molly's hair was so neat.

I never saw the smiles,
The looks they gave each other,
Just the two together,
I felt so far from smiles.

I loved that day!
The way we laughed,
The way we splashed,
I loved that day!

Hollie Farrow (13)
Colston's Girls' School, Bristol

That Swallow

(Based on 'Private Peaceful' by Michael Morpurgo)

Swooping and swaying
Jumping and playing
Out in the open he went
I'll miss him, my father
Forever and after
But time can never relent.

Alice Webber (12)
Colston's Girls' School, Bristol

The Best Year

Which year was the best?
Year 5 was the best, because . . .
I had amazing friends.
My best friend was Caitlin, yes, Caitlin.
You could do near enough everything with her.
Christy was fashionable, yes, fashionable describes her well,
Seeing she loved singing and clothes.
Year 5 was the best.
The lessons were made fun.
My favourite lesson was sport, yes, sport.
You did nearly everything you intended in a term.
Maths was easy, yes, easy suits maths,
Seeing I always finished first.
Year 5 was the best,
The teachers were really nice.
Miss Fairweather would let you do nearly everything, yes, everything.
I loved it in Miss Fairweather's class,
I thought it was amazing.
Mrs Williamson was a pleasure, yes, a pleasure.
Seeing she was the nicest deputy head I knew.
That sums up Year 5, I thought Year 5 was great.

Emily Wright (10)
Colston's Girls' School, Bristol

What Is War?

What is war?
Does it makes us happy, sad?
In the end what does it do?
Does it make us glad we have won?

What is war?
Does it kill our friends, family?
In the end what does it do?
Does it make us sad we have lost?

War is bad.
It kills our friends, family.
In the end it carries on.
No one loses and no one wins.

What is war?
Does it break our hearts, heads?
In the end what does it do?
Does it worry us that we might die?

What is war?
Do we go home joyful we have killed men?
In the end what does it do?
Does it make us happy we've got more land?

War is bad.
It ruins our world.
In the end it carries on.
We all go home with broken hearts.

Rose Juliet (11)
Colston's Girls' School, Bristol

Friends

When someone new comes into view
Could it be that your feelings show?
Or maybe it's just something else
That I just do not know.
Happiness or sadness or another emotion that you feel
But beware that what you feel is always for real.

For example, I have a friend called Yasmin
Whose face is as white as snow
She has been my friend for many years now
For I was there forever with her, oh how I miss her now
She was a Jamaican flower, proud of her culture,
Something I adored about her and inspired me always.

Though I have not seen her since we both fell apart
She moved back to Jamaica and that broke my heart
I think about her every day and how we would have changed.
I hope I can see her someday soon
Before she fades away from my mind
Oh I hope I can see her before I leave her behind.
Or is there something else I can do?

Mariam Olatidoye (11)
Colston's Girls' School, Bristol

Woodberry Down

Woodberry Down was really fun,
Out of all the things we did, archery was the best.
Orienteering was a bit boring, doing all the clues.
Besides that, everything was fun.
Really exciting for two days,
Really fun to stay away from home,
You know, with all my friends.
Down in the woods were thistles,
Once I got tangled in them.
When I got untangled, we had a laugh,
Nothing was better than Woodberry Down.

Lois Linter
Colston's Girls' School, Bristol

Life Goes On For Some

I walked in my house
It felt lonely, quiet, empty
I wandered upstairs
I couldn't find him
Upstairs, downstairs or outside
My life was ruined
My heart was pounding
Days, weeks, months went past
Till one day I found out
He had been murdered, killed, slaughtered
By my own parents
I felt hurt, betrayed, left out
Suddenly, I went into shock
Memories of him flashed in my mind
The good, the bad and the fun
My life had failed but now I know
I can dream of him on his own.

Nicole Morris (14)
Oakmead College of Technology, Bournemouth

Spectacles Of A Mute

To you
I'm a car without wheels,
I'm a bird without wings,
I'm a fish without sea,
Nothing special, a freak,
An outcast, an empty gormless shell.

To me
I'm a firework waiting to explode,
To show my beautiful bright lights.
I long for you, the perfect, the normal, the great
To watch beyond the cold empty shell
And feel the warmth of my burning fire of personality.

Caroline Allen (16)
Oakmead College of Technology, Bournemouth

Never Forget That Day

I will never forget that day,
I can remember it so clearly.
Dad awoke me early one summer's morning,
He was taking me out for the day.
I asked him where we were going -
He said to wait and see.
We got in the car, I peeked through the windows.
My tiny eyes could not believe the mass of colour.
Clouds in the sky, fields of sunflowers.
I had never been here before, the country.
We pulled up to a river, Dad said, 'We are here!'
The expression on my face instantly dropped.
'Don't look so upset, come on,' he said.
We walked side by side to the river edge.
There was a present on the floor, wrapped in pink paper.
'It's for you,' he whispered in my ear.
I opened it, it was a rounders set.
Dad knew how much I wanted one,
We played all afternoon, laughter and giggles filled my ears.
The sun began to set, 'Time to go,' Dad said.
I ran up to him and gave him a massive hug,
'Thanks Dad, I have had a great day!'
Next morning he was gone and I never saw him again.

Helen McCann (14)
Oakmead College of Technology, Bournemouth

A Life As A Leaf

When I wake up I look at the weather
Am I going to be blown around
All hot and shrivelled or maybe even cold?
I think, *what shall I do?*
What am I?

Like a child with lots of energy, full of life and fun
Lots of pretty colours and such a feeling of life
Same feelings, either hot or cold.
What am I?

Today it looks like I'm going to be blown around
Oh no, hold on tight, here it comes.
Whee, that was fun, here it comes again.
I hope I don't get blown away.
What am I?

It starts to rain; I'm going to get wet,
Be very cold and very, very wet.
I think I might fall off.
Please no, I don't want to fall.
It gets harder, pitter-patter, *whoosh!*
What am I?

My last clue then you have to guess.
I am about to fall off, here I go.
I'm ready to be trodden on,
Whoosh, I'm gone by.
What am I?

Nicole Taylor (15)
Oakmead College of Technology, Bournemouth

No One's Perfect

Why did you say
The things you said?
Why was it always my fault?
You said you heard me
When I moaned and cried,
But why did you not listen?
You said it's unfair
That you are stuck,
Where you are
With who you are.
You think it was fair for me?
Why did you ignore me
When I said I was hurt?
Could I not bleed too?
Could I not stumble and fall
And cry and scar?
Was I not a replica of you?
All I ever wanted was the affection I deserved
But it was all reserved for him.
He who always got what he wanted.
Cuddles, love, kind words.
Now it's too late.
I gave you your chance to make it right,
Now, it's your fault.
I will hang around the house forever reminding you
No one's perfect.

Victoria Oliver (16)
Oakmead College of Technology, Bournemouth

Turn The Time

Think of the possibilities,
People's abilities,
If Man could turn back time.

Lives could be saved,
Prayers could be answered,
Problems braved
And future known.

There would be no poverty,
Crisis abolished,
No danger,
No trouble,
No homes demolished.

What would you do if you could turn the time?
I would spend some more on this poem of mine.
Just take a minute to stop and think,
What really matters?

Don't waste time
Or you'll waste your life.

But until it has run out
Do not wait,
Because if you could turn back time
You would never be late.

Jamie Anderson (14)
Oakmead College of Technology, Bournemouth

Rachel's Date Of A Lifetime

From the second my phone beeped, I knew who it was!
The butterflies in my belly went wild.
It was him.
We arranged the date and I couldn't wait.

When the day finally came I was a nervous wreck.
My hair blew in the wind as I waited outside the glamorous restaurant
And then I saw him!
His handsome, tall figure strutted towards me.
He put his arms around me and kissed me lightly on the lips!
A kiss that could melt even the coldest of ice!

In the restaurant we gazed lovingly at each other across the table.
I was in Heaven!
Soon enough the date was over and I was left reminiscing over
the night's events,
Never have I felt so safe, so happy, so adored!

Tanya Brierley (17)
Oakmead College of Technology, Bournemouth

Life Of A Chair

At first I was soft, plump and proud,
Watching the people pass and look, testing what I was like,
Trusting me to support them, asking me to comfort them.
The arms I provided were strong, they stood outward forever
But never ached, holding the souls that longed to recover.
As the clock ticked my skin aged, my stitches burst and I sunk
within myself.
People never bothered to look anymore, stare or admire what
I once was.
They always put my appearance first, always before my purpose.
Now it is too late but I will remember the fun we had with the parents
and theirs before.
I may be old but they will remember me as their supporting friend.

Rachel Moore (16)
Oakmead College of Technology, Bournemouth

Great Memories

The first signs of winter
Were on the way
Very cold mornings
And days that were grey.

It brought snow and frost
That stayed for weeks,
Frosty grounds
And very cold feet.

Snowball fights started out
With children laughing, beginning to shout.
Eventually the kids gave up at midday
Because more frost was coming their way.

Next time in winter
It will be cold again,
With frost and snow and cries of cheer
Winter's definitely my favourite time of year.

Ben Gartshore (15)
Oakmead College of Technology, Bournemouth

The Days

Gone were the days of laughter,
Those you will always remember.
Times of love and happiness,
That will stay with you forever.

Never forget those days,
Full of happiness and sun.
Playing in fresh fields,
Those were the days of fun.

Though the days are gone,
Keep them sparkling like gems.
Look back over the happy times,
And just don't you ever forget them.

Jessica Moulden (14)
Oakmead College of Technology, Bournemouth

Who Would You Call When You Need Help?

Who would you call when you need help?
Who is there twenty-four hours a day?
Driving to a murder
Rock hits your car
Helping the community, insults are thrown.

Who would you call when you need help?
Who is there when no one else is?
Drunken drivers
But you're the scum
Saving lives
But who notices?

Who would you call when you need help?
Who will save you when no one else will?
What would you do if we never came?
Who will come running if we don't?

Who would you call when you need help?
Who would be your saviour?
Why should we help when no one cares?
What would you do if we weren't there?

Who would you call when you need help?
Who would be the one to make it right?
Why should we help your kidnapped child?
Why should we help your stabbed partner?

Who would you call when you need help?
Who would be there for us when we need it?
When will be the day people take note?
Realising we're here to help.

Charlotte Franklin (14)
Oakmead College of Technology, Bournemouth

The Concatenation Of Life

The start, an explosion of life.
Leaping from your burrow,
You gaze at a scene of pain, drama and blood.
The screams reside and comfort swells
Into the eerie insurance from which you feed.
The hollow happiness hallucinates your
Growth, watching with blind eyes.
Growth, walking on still legs.
Growth, speaking with muted lips.
You age as your age began.

Days dissolving into years
And every season robbing from your treasury.
Dust gathers on the events
Which soar like stars
And die with a heat of passion and fire.
Evolution escalates, elongating into
Progress, learning what is not taught.
Progress, working until incomplete.
Progress, resting until you expire.
The hidden truth of what you could have done.

And so the comforting blanket
Begins to crease.
Your mind wanders
At the abstraction of a lifetime.
The sun hits the coastline
With a powerful profanity, it's profound
Realisation, you've lived your life.
Realisation, you're told it's not yours.
Realisation, you begin not to care.
For you hold dear the memories you bear.

Mark Dyer (15)
Oakmead College of Technology, Bournemouth

I Wish

I wish they wouldn't look at me that way,
See that inside I'm just like them.
I have a mind to think,
Even though I can't speak out loud.

I wish they wouldn't look at me that way,
I'm just a normal person really.
Why can't they see I'm just like them?
I have a body, arms, legs, we're all alike in ways.

I wish they wouldn't look at me that way,
Their facial expression tells everything.
The way they all feel sorry for me,
Why can't we all be treated the same?

I wish they wouldn't look at me that way,
They don't even talk to me anymore.
It's not my fault, I try to tell them
But what's the point, they wouldn't listen.

I wish they wouldn't look at me that way,
Please just stop at least once and awhile
Just to talk to me,
Because I will answer you, just as long as you listen.

Charlotte Sharp (14)
Oakmead College of Technology, Bournemouth

Will They Die Tonight?

Hovering in a dirty corner
Whimpering, crying, hurting
What did they do?
Nothing, absolutely nothing.

Beaten to a quivering pulp
Thrown like a rag doll
Is this what life is?
No, but that's what they've got.

Will they die tonight?
Will they be saved?
Helped from the darkness?
Is that what they crave?

Save them from it
The hell that they live
Save the children
From their lonely misery.

Kate Drummond (14)
Oakmead College of Technology, Bournemouth

If Only I Could Turn Back Time

If only I could turn back time,
There's many things to change.
Like the time I fell out with my friends
And that's why my life was a struggle,
If only I could turn back time.

If only time could be turned back,
There's many things to change.
Like the time I laughed at a rather large girl
And that's why school was difficult.
If only I could turn back time.

If only I could turn back time,
There's many things to change.
Like the time I upset my best friend
Now that's something I really regret.
If only I could turn back time.

If only time could be turned back,
There's many things to change.
Like the time family members died
I wish I could bring them back.
If only I could turn back time.

If only I could turn back time,
There's many things to change.
There's so many things that I regret
I wish I didn't do.
If only I could turn back time.

Carrianne Chandler (14)
Oakmead College of Technology, Bournemouth

Give Someone A Voice Who Cannot Speak

I wish I could tell everyone
I'm not happy
Because it's my birthday
But no one remembered.
So I open my mouth
But nothing comes out
Then it makes me sad
That I cannot tell them.
So I weep in silence
Where no one will hear
And I think to myself
And try to cheer myself up.
When I get back
I hear a cheer
I scream out loud
For everyone to hear.
I jump for joy
Everyone standing there
All my friends
All around here,
They did remember my birthday
Now I'm happy again.

Lauren Ridout (14)
Oakmead College of Technology, Bournemouth

Time Traveller

If you could turn back time
What would you do?
Go to the past or the future
And be the next Dr Who?

Travel to distant lands
Where dinosaurs there will be,
Beware though
As these ones roam free!

A flash in time
A cry in space,
Till you arrive
At a new place.

A time where no one is safe
Men are sent away to fight,
While at home the bombs are dropping
The men abroad fight for right!

A flash in time
A cry in space,
Till you arrive
At a new place.

An era of revolution
Where motor cars fly,
But watch out for the robots
When they pass you by!

If you could turn back time
What would you do?
Go to the past or the future
And be the next Dr Who?

Stephanie Teal (14)
Oakmead College of Technology, Bournemouth

The Last Day Of Term

The beginning of the day takes place,
You wake up and you look a disgrace.
You put on your tie and rush down the stairs,
The last day of term is always unfair.

You walk at last through the gate,
Then you realise that you're late!
The place is deserted, no one's around,
You rush to your lesson, through the school grounds.

Suddenly a familiar sound you hear
A sound, right now, that you dread and fear.
You turn, you twist, the bell has rung,
This signifies that the first lesson's begun.

You take your seat at the back,
You get what you need from your rucksack.
You take out your pen, and your pencil too,
But distracted again, there's chewing gum on your shoe.

The bell no longer inspires fear
Because its sound is what you're waiting to hear.
And the joyous emotions that it brings
When the bell goes and very loudly rings.

Finally, lunchtime has gone and ended,
The model you made before lunch shall be mended.
The hour goes on, and on and on,
The teacher speaks out, 'Bye and be gone.'

Coming near is the end of the day,
There's no more time to run and play.
Darkness has come, the moon is alone,
Because the last day of term has gone.

Matthew Legg (14)
Oakmead College of Technology, Bournemouth

As I Walked

As I walked up to the trampoline,
My heart went thud, thud, thud.
Thirty seconds later, first routine finished.
8.5, 8.4, 8.3, 8.4.

A big smile appeared across my face,
On the board, '1st Katy I'anson'
Back to focusing, second routine to finish.
Eyes closed, visualise routine.

As I walked up to the trampoline,
My heart went thud, thud, thud.
Thirty seconds later, second routine finished.
8.1, 7.9, 8.2, 8.1, 8.3.

An even bigger smile appeared, if possible,
Name didn't move. '1st Katy I'anson'
Focusing, final routine to do.
Head down, visualising routine.

As I walked up to the trampoline,
My heart went thud, thud, thud.
Thirty seconds later, final routine finished.
8.1, 8.2, 8.1, 8.3, 8.2.

Emotions running through, like a hawk soaring through the sky,
'British National Champion Katy I'anson.'
Was announced, I stood on the podium
Cameras flashing, people cheering, me smiling.

This was the beginning of my career,
This was the happiest day of my life.

Katy I'anson (15)
Oakmead College of Technology, Bournemouth

The Race

I'm in the car and it's starting to rain
The brakes are glowing bright red.
The car starts to slide like a snake over ice.
Spray from the car in front is making me blind.
I'm catching the car in front, he begins to slow.
Yes, yes I am past to move into third place.
Oh no, I have spun around Nick, his back passes me.

It's time to enter the pits, visibility is really bad,
The noise intense like a raging bull.
The pressure of the tyres is reduced,
I'm out again and in sixth.
Nick has spun around, the yellow flag's out.
I can see the car in front; he is my teammate,
I need to get past to get a chance of winning.

The green flag is out; I throw the car into the corner,
Like a toy car, I am gaining on him, catching him by every second.
I drive up the inside, he moves in slowly.
He nearly touches me but I escape without a scratch.
I press on to catch the next car in third.

The rain is clearing and the sun is appearing, the day is looking up.
The car in third is slowing for the corner, I don't slow.
I need to pass him, I slip and slide, I must pass.
He slows again; I launch the car down a small gap,
He turns in and hits me, I spin and stall.
I can't get it started; the day isn't looking up,
That's my race over.

Carl Penny (15)
Oakmead College of Technology, Bournemouth

The Youths You Never See

Youths standing on the streets
Hoods up on their hooded tops
Smoking, drinking and shouting abuse
Is this the image we have of our youth?
How come we only see the bad
And never see the other side?
The smart, the helpful and the brave,
The ones that will go far.

A little old lady walking down the street
Helpless, like a bird with a broken wing.
They would expect a hooded youth
With a cigarette in their hand
And a knife in their pocket
To mug this helpless woman
As if they were a prowling cat
But they are wrong!

What about the youths that care
The ones that would respect this woman
The ones that are bullied
The ones that are scared
The ones that these prowling cats prey upon just for fun
The youths you never see
The youths that are dead.

Kurt Redrup (15)
Oakmead College of Technology, Bournemouth

Blind Man

You're the only one I can trust,
I can feel you, hear you, smell you.
For all I know you could be a monster
A villain, an evil person with a sick mind.
But you're not, I know.

For all I know
You could be ugly, scary, freaky, grotesque.
But you're not, I know.
For all I know you're not real,
Just a figment of my imagination.
But you're not, I know.

For all I know
You could be a talking parrot or a robot even.
But you're not, I know.
For all I know
That voice of yours isn't real, it's just an impression.
But it's not, I know.

For all I know
You could be an impostor, a trickster.
But you're not, I know.
For all I know
You could be a lovely, beautiful, real person.
And you are, I know.

David Foord (15)
Oakmead College of Technology, Bournemouth

My Poem

If I were to turn back time
What would yesterday and tomorrow bring?
The land could be filled with new creations
That we have never encountered before.
Who knows what would walk the Earth.
There could be eight-legged freaks jumping,
Dinosaurs in the dense jungle roaring,
How loud would they be?
We simply don't know,
There are so many mysteries.

If we were encountered by the imaginary,
If we could fly into outer space,
Who knows what there would be?
If we went back millions of years
The world would be so different.
It's just too brain-annoying to wonder,
Why were we created?
Where are we from?
Who knows?
No one, the possibilities are endless.

Dean Derbyshire (15)
Oakmead College of Technology, Bournemouth

Good Times, Great Memories

Life is full of good times
Life is full of bad times
The memories are often jumbled
Good for worse
Bad for better
Each as valuable as the last.

Experiences make us who we are
A lesson learnt is a lesson lived
But each makes us better
Our memories last forever
As the stars that look upon us
Each holding secrets
Each holding thoughts.

But, if they die
They will not be forgotten
As its existence will last forever
As its existence has made our future
And our future will bring good times
Our future will bring bad times
But it will not bring great memories.

Alistair Cannings (15)
Oakmead College of Technology, Bournemouth

The New Arrival

When I heard the news I could hardly contain my excitement,
We had waited desperately for good news
Then we were told that my baby sister had been born.

When I went to visit, the nurse brought her through,
There she was lying in her cot; she had beautiful brown hair,
Big blue eyes, as clear as water and tiny hands and feet.
I picked her up and she was as light and as delicate as a feather.

I couldn't believe what I saw; she was just so cute, cuddly
and carefree.
I sat there staring at her for ages; she was the perfect baby sister.
She glared at me with her big eyes, then slowly drifted back
off to sleep.

Snap, snap went the camera, family gathering round, just looking
at the baby,
Mixed emotions running through me,
Happiness, joy and excitement, couldn't believe what had happened!

When at home you would never know she was there,
Millions of toys, loud noises, lots of beeps, honks and baby giggles!
You really couldn't live without her!

When I heard the news I could hardly contain my excitement,
We had waited desperately for good news
Then we were told that my baby sister had been born.

Lauren Clark (15)
Oakmead College of Technology, Bournemouth

I Want To Be Noticed

I sit there every day
In pain, in agony
I sit there being ignored
Hoping that one day I will get noticed.

I am sat there in my armchair
Wondering if I will get noticed
I stare out the window
Hoping that one day I will get noticed.

People walk past my window
They see me and look away
I shout at them in agony
Hoping that one day I will get noticed.

I sit there like a shrivelled up rotten apple
Unable to move, unable to speak up
Wondering if one day, one day, I will get noticed.

Then that day happened
I was noticed
Able to move, able to speak up,
I was given my chance, I hope you get yours.

Alex Gibbs (15)
Oakmead College of Technology, Bournemouth

Rockology 101

When God got bored one day
Of all the cold and quiet nights and heavenly mist
God got out his Gibson SG
And started strumming with His right wrist.

The sound was heavy but yet sweet
As if a melodic chant from angels' wings
But from the tip of the SG an orange glow appeared
As planets emerged out of the darkness
All moshing to the heavenly chorus of the gods.

God had warmed up, now it was time to shred
As He started His mind-melting run
His fingers moved faster and faster
Until He got past the point of no return
He shouted, 'Let there be light'
His huge swishy white hair flapped everywhere
As His axe recoiled as a massive rocking fireball
Shot out of His holy SG illuminating
The heavens as the planets moshed around the sun
To the heavenly chorus of the gods.

God was pleased with what He had created
He smiled and nodded His glowing head
He whispered under His breath, 'My best ever work ever
But something's missing'
So He started to play something else
And suddenly Man appeared on Earth all over the globe
Happy and smiley for all to see God shouted
'Here, take My holy rocking harp and rock for all that will be!'

Jacob Stone (15)
Oakmead College of Technology, Bournemouth

Windy Wendy

I'm a tree called Windy Wendy
And when I stand up the wind makes me all bendy.
I have a very long trunk
And when I reach I look like a big hunk.
My leaves are all crusty
So I add some oil so they don't go rusty.
Also my branches are thin
Just like a pin.
I have long roots
And I wear big fat boots.
The soil around me is soft
Just like candyfloss.
When it starts to rain
I cover up with pain.
When the sun comes out
I start to shout.
When the squirrels come to feed
They bury themselves in-between the weeds.
The birds will land on my branches
But they always take chances.
I look forward to spring
When my leaves open and go ding, ding, ding.
When the winter falls
My body changes and goes tall.
People walk past me
And they always say excuse me.
Owls nest inside me because they want to keep warm
They only do it when there is a storm.

Chloe Lewis (15)
Oakmead College of Technology, Bournemouth

Lost Loves And Get Backs

He goes round with a knife in his hand
Ready to stab you in the heart,
There's no regret when the deed is done,
At least they're out of their pain.

He tries to make you live in sorrow,
But the tears come on too strong,
They just can't stand the horror
Of living, having to face him every day.

He's a backstabber and he's nasty,
He deserves much less than he gets,
They all wish he was dead,
But he's too proud of what he's done.

He now lies under the ground
Like a monster destined for Hell,
As he lay there cold, crazy and crying,
The parents cheered for joy.

Hayley Cuff (14)
Oakmead College of Technology, Bournemouth

If I Went Back

If only I could go back in time
What would I do?
Would I do good or bad
By changing history?

Would I be able to stop a war before it began
And save the lives of millions?

If I went back,
Could I prevent disease and save the lives
Of many women, men and children?

If I went back,
Could I stop a disaster before it happened
And save many innocent lives?

Now if only I could go back in time.

Robbie Board (15)
Oakmead College of Technology, Bournemouth

Goodnight Dad

The last few days I spent with you
I did not know what I should do,
Should I stay and speak aloud
Or simply hide out in the crowd.
Your body lying hopelessly
All you'd need was love from me,
All the love that I did give
Did not work or make you live.
I cry alone remembering
Those three days, yes, everything,
You were just quietly resting there
All I could do was stand and stare.
I needed you to just wake up
I thought that you would not give up,
Suddenly you closed your eyes
I did not get to say goodbye.
I held my tears with all my might
Just for now I'll say goodnight.

Sophia Peutherer (14)
Torquay Grammar School for Girls, Torquay

Through That Door

Through that door
Are distant memories,
Howls of agony from the war
The fading picture of a late general
And his army dropping lifelessly to their knees and dying.

Through that door
Is the tear-stained face of a girl
She's lost her father
And her mother still grieves.

Through that door
Is a bundle of joy
A family who could celebrate for years to come,
A baby boy granting his first wish, a great big smile.

Zoe Lumley (13)
Torquay Grammar School for Girls, Torquay

The Flower

Flowers come in different shapes and sizes,
Different colours like red or blue,
But this flower is strange.

Its brightness fills even the darkest spaces,
Its scent is extraordinary too,
It makes you joyful all the time,
Even in the most frightening.

Its stem is greener than an evergreen tree
And also blooms all year round.
The sight of this flower is so beautiful
You have to shield your eyes.

In winter no snow covers this flower
It's different from the background,
No age grows on this flower
It stands there all year round.

In summer its brightness, its beauty
Is seen from miles on end.
In spring it blooms like all the other flowers
In autumn it's surrounded by leaves.

Flowers come in different shapes and sizes
Different colours like red or blue
But that flower was strange.

Savanna Bonstow (11)
Torquay Grammar School for Girls, Torquay

Rejection

Why should we include someone in our lives because they are
                                                    so different?
So, we turned our backs on that stray, Jimmy Jones.
It is only now that I realise as I've grown old and wiser
That if we had included poor Jimmy Jones
He wouldn't have committed suicide.

Josephine Hanrott (11)
Torquay Grammar School for Girls, Torquay

Invisible

There is a girl with no name,
No voice, no friends and she doesn't play games.
Everyone pushes past her on their way,
So she never goes out to play.
She will sit on her own in the cloakroom,
Praying and praying a friend will come soon.
All the girls group up together,
But her? No, no, never.

We all know the girl who is sitting on her own,
We have all felt like her when we're all alone.
So why doesn't anyone say,
'Hey you! Come over and play.'
But for this girl all on her own,
When she is with her family she doesn't feel alone.

In the future when the girl is older,
She has become much, much bolder.
Now she is a superstar,
On stage singing, *'Hurrah, hurrah!'*
So all I have to say to you,
Think about that girl, it could become you too!

As for the girl who is a global superstar,
She is stopping bullying wide and far.
The girl has a name and it is a lovely name
Nobody for planets has the same.
I am going to let you guess her name,
The girl who now has all the fame.
Bullying is bad!

Charlotte Walmsley (11)
Torquay Grammar School for Girls, Torquay

Me@Cats - Haiku

We have features, we
Have problems, we have a life
Mostly we're unique.

Amy Lett (11)
Torquay Grammar School for Girls, Torquay

Colours That Can't Be Seen

The magical colours of life
Are the ones that you cannot see.
You cannot see them in the mountains,
Or anywhere else you have been.

You may sing with all the voices
Or dance with all the leaves,
But you may never paint
With any colours like these.

It is not to be seen by any human
Who in life has sinned.
Only creatures of purity
Can see colours of the wind.

Katie Girow (13)
Torquay Grammar School for Girls, Torquay

Bullied

I sit in the corner
Alone and sad
Emotionally exhausted
My feelings hurt
A relentless pain.

It's not my fault I'm different
But they like that.

I didn't want to come to school
I didn't want to face it
Mother said I have to though
I won't let it bother me
I won't let them see
But I'm not the only one
'Cause there are other people just like me.

Sophia Nikolaou (12)
Torquay Grammar School for Girls, Torquay

Dreamszzzz

Dreams are magical, amazing and weird
Sometimes nightmares of things you've feared.
Other times you adventure around
Finding lots of things that you've found.
When you awake to reality
You forget all the strange things you see.

Dreams are magical, amazing and weird
Sometimes nightmares of things you've feared.
Monsters and ghosts haunt you all night through
Where creepy skeletons and ghouls live too
When you awake to reality
You forget all the strange things that you see.

Dreams are magical, amazing and weird
Sometimes nightmares of things you've feared.
Dreams can feel so real and true
But life should be more important to you.
And when you awake to reality
You forget all the strange things that you see.

Constance Collier-Qureshy (11)
Torquay Grammar School for Girls, Torquay

The Sea In A Storm

The sea in a storm is like raging anger
Brewing inside and then letting it rip
The white horses galloping on top of the waves
Crashing into a passing ship.

The sea in a storm is like a stampede of mermaids
In a race to see who can reach the shore first
A large bubble that somebody's blown
Floating around, ready to burst.

The sea in a storm is like a lion's roar
Loud at first, then quietening down.
Thunderbolts and lightning streaks
Everyone waiting for the sound to drown.

Emily Roberts (12)
Torquay Grammar School for Girls, Torquay

My Mum's Party

On Saturday my mum was forty,
I'm afraid to say she was very naughty,
She danced all night until she was giddy
And ended up walking like a right old biddy!

The room was filled with lots of balloons,
And knives and forks and even spoons.
She had lots to drink and plenty to eat,
But by the end of the night she had sore feet.

With lots of people from old to young
The room was filled with tons of fun,
We had raspberry cheesecake and chocolate cake
But when we went to get some, we were too late.

A bit of cake filled with cream
That made you dream and dream
And so we came to the end of the night
And there were never any fights.

Lilly Bertram (12)
Torquay Grammar School for Girls, Torquay

Lights Out

L eaving light behind, heading into darkness
I magination runs amok, dreams flowing through my mind
G oing down a twisting path, choosing random trails
H uffing and puffing, hearing footsteps following me
T errified, I look around but no one is there
S truggling on through my fear, unsure of every turn

O verwhelmed, excited and yet petrified, uncontrolled
U nder a bridge, over a river, almost out of this nightmare
T ired but awake, haunted but happy, I am finally free.

Sophie Parsons (12)
Torquay Grammar School for Girls, Torquay

Seasons

So many lambs and chicks and calves,
Spring is full of so many laughs.
Children playing and having fun,
In the fields with the warm spring sun.

Bees, butterflies and summer aromas abound,
Crowds on sandy beaches, ice cream all around.
Sun blazing, children swimming and the heat,
The deep blue sea to cool our feet.

Rusty coloured leaves fall upon the ground,
The cool autumn breeze brushes them around.
Animals gather their food in heaps,
Ready for their winter sleeps.

Cold, frosty winter blues,
Snowflakes fall upon our shoes.
Trees bare, rivers covered in ice,
Christmas, sledges, snowmen so very nice!

Megan Duff (11)
Torquay Grammar School for Girls, Torquay

A Poem

I knew you when you were younger,
Younger than before.
I knew you when you were older,
Older, wiser, mature.

Days pass as years fly,
Going quickly in your eyes.
Sudden changes appear,
In weird ways but slowly disappear.

Through all the good times and the bad,
Kept happy, joyful and glad.
For when that days comes you will see,
The real child inside of me.

Danielle Orrell (11)
Torquay Grammar School for Girls, Torquay

Skiing

A clean, clear ski slope,
Cold, fresh and white,
Until the first skier comes
And slices through like a knife.

The sensation of flying
When down a slope you ski
It must be how a bird feels
Flying light and free.

Going up in a chair lift
To mountains high as high,
When I'm up there I almost feel like
I could touch the sky!

Then when you get to the bottom
So tired, you could snooze,
You've had enough for one day
But you'll be back soon!

Emily Melluish (11)
Torquay Grammar School for Girls, Torquay

If I Could Turn Back The Hands Of Time

If I could turn back the hands of time
Would you still be mine
To love and to hold
Through sickness and through health?
I love you and always will
I miss the thrill you gave me
I'll look back and remember the things we used to do
Oh, if I could turn back the hands of time
Then I'd be with you and you'd be forever mine.

Hannah Gill (13)
Torquay Grammar School for Girls, Torquay

Roaring

Roaring, roaring,
Like a lion in a cage!
Roaring, roaring,
Like someone in a rage!

Run, run,
Get away from it!
Run, run
Away.

Roaring, roaring,
Like a lion in a cage!
Roaring, roaring,
Like someone in a rage!

I'm running, running,
Running away.
Running, running,
Away.

Roaring, roaring,
Like a lion in a cage!
Roaring, roaring,
Like someone in a rage!

Where is it? What is it?
Why, why,
Why is it after me?

Sukayna Zayer (11)
Torquay Grammar School for Girls, Torquay

A New World

It was cold,
Rain tears streamed down my face,
It was a storm,
Fierce to embrace.

The thunder struck so loud,
Again and again,
I knew a new world
Was about to begin.

Trees fell,
Cold became hell,
Children cried,
Parents by their sides.

Then suddenly the flashes stopped,
God's coughing soon calmed down,
And children all fell silent,
Parents left with a frown.

So black was the sky,
The panic was all gone,
And quiet was the night
All its hard work done.

Imogen Uniacke (12)
Torquay Grammar School for Girls, Torquay

A World In A Word

My backdrop and surroundings, everything fake,
All was captured by Shakespeare and Blake.
Many former writers transformed my home,
From a distant dream to a dazzling dome.

My world is filled with wondrous words,
Fashioning everything from bees to birds.
Without these words, nothing would be there,
Nowhere to look, no one to stare.

So why do our words shape the Earth,
Was it not good enough after its birth?
We've made it change from dull to bright,
To show what we want through what we write.

We've searched for a phrase to explain what we do,
But no one could find it, not me, nor you.
Millions came with suggestions in herds
And then we discovered, we're away with words.

Hollie Dennison (13)
Torquay Grammar School for Girls, Torquay

Fuzzy

Would we have tried harder if we both knew
Or would we have tried less?
Would we still be together
Or have parted even quicker?
Is there something else we should have said
Or was there not much more we could do?
Life is a funny thing
It leaves you all warm and fuzzy
But if you don't tell people how you feel
Hearts might be broken by the words unspoken.

Rebecca Polding (14)
Torquay Grammar School for Girls, Torquay

Abused, Confused

My thoughts are banished, opinions gone
My mind is buzzing but my world's undone
I'm drowning in my tears, a waterfall of despair
I'm giving up on breathing but no one seems to care

My mother hates me, my father left
I tell my sister that I'm hurting but she acts as though she's deaf
I wish I was a bird so I could fly away from here
But chains of strong emotions still bind me to this year

A sea of thoughts, a world of judgements
Is engulfing me and dragging my spirit
Down into the depths of despondent death
I wish I could just live being me and savour every breath

My strength is dying, my muscles ache
I desire a different world every morning when I wake
One where she couldn't torment me
And a world where my soul is free.

Abigail Lowe (13)
Torquay Grammar School for Girls, Torquay

Lights Out

L eft alone in a mystical dream
I nside the depths of a hidden realm
G azing into the field of slumber
H ow to find the place I seek
T o stumble and ponder through the deep
S earching for the door back

O n track but never there
U biquitous paths to follow
T o the creak that wakes me.

Holly Badger (12)
Torquay Grammar School for Girls, Torquay

All Alone

When walking along
There was no turning back,
No second chances,
No second crack.
Never have I felt so lonely,
Never have I felt so cold,
Never have I felt like my world was crashing down,
Never has this feeling grown old.
But as I was walking
All I could do was cry,
And sing to myself
As the cars whizzed by.
Where was I going?
Did I even know?
I had my plan:
Just go with the flow.
But when I thought about it
What could I do?
My mind was exploding into a million pieces,
My whole life was going to change
And leave a million creases.
But this is no bit of paper
Which you can screw up and retry,
This was my whole world, my life,
If only this poem was a lie.
So there I was.
All alone,
No friend in the world.
I'd lost my home.

Juliet Wheeler (13)
Torquay Grammar School for Girls, Torquay

I Will Remember

The times we played in the sand
And sang songs to our mum and dad
So now you are gone I can't say
I will remember our games

When we rode up and down for hours
Pretending our scooter could fly
They could take us anywhere we wanted
I will remember our flights

I say this hoping you can hear me
You're in a place I can't visit
I hope that you can hear me when I say
I will remember our talks

All those times we rode our bikes
To what we used to think was Australia
Never tiring of that same place
I will remember our adventures

I never had time to say I am sorry
For all those times that were never solved
Yet we were still friends without that simple word
I will remember our fights

You will always exist in my heart
I will see you one day in the future
Till that time I can only say
I will remember.

Kate Guppy (13)
Torquay Grammar School for Girls, Torquay

How I Fell

You play with my heart and mess up my head
I believe everything you've ever said
It feels like a trap that I fell for
I'll keep on falling till I hit the floor
I call for you but you walk away
All I want is for you to stay
I reach out with everything I've got
I need you because you're all that I'm not
If this isn't right then why do I bleed?
I've told you, it's you that I need
If I'm not with you, you're with me
Forever, always, how I want it to be
Because you light me up and lift me high
Higher than I've seen, higher than the sky
Will you ever pick me up and tell me it will be okay?
If yes, then when is that day?
If no, I guess goodbye
I'll fall and for the last time fly.

Keira Mayne (13)
Torquay Grammar School for Girls, Torquay

Three Different Worlds

Lying beneath the sun, amongst the acacia trees,
As one with nature, the birds and the bees,
In a country that is dry, where it seldom rains,
A country of peace, the African plains.

A walk through the jungle, humid and mild,
Where animals thrive, growing fierce and wild,
From the ancient trees, where monkeys are curled
To the damp rich earth, the forest of the world.

The streets are full of cars, pumping pollution,
As I drive through them, I make a contribution,
We are killing the world with factories and smoke,
We must repair the gap or there will be no hope.

Jasmine Hogg (11)
Torquay Grammar School for Girls, Torquay

Lights Out

A prisoner isolated and confined,
Continuous thoughts circling in his mind
Capturing and trapping him
In another sleepless night
His dreams and hopes running out of sight.

Hours have passed but he is still caught
Stranded, drowning in his unwanted thoughts.
Innocent in mind, guilty in body.
He is alone.
He is isolated.
He is trapped.
He sits motionless.

Wiping the unwelcome tears from his eye,
Inside of him he secretly dies.
Having only the velvety darkness
Encasing him for comfort, for advice
He thinks about sleep and then thinks twice.

A time for reflection,
A time that is thoughtful
The only time the fearless can become the fearful
After lights out.

Camilla Wakeford (12)
Torquay Grammar School for Girls, Torquay

My World

I picture my world relaxed and at peace.
I picture my world with war to cease.
I picture my world for black and white to be as one.
I picture my world for everyone to have fun.
I picture my world where starvation will stop.
I picture a world where there are trees we can't chop.
I picture my world for global warming to disappear.
I picture a world where there is peace and music my children can hear.

Madeleine Whatmore (11)
Torquay Grammar School for Girls, Torquay

Lights Out

A blink. A flash. I turn about
Before I know it the lights are out.
A looming darkness is all I know
Before it snuffs the warming glow
A trip. A slip. I'm on my knees
Between the shadows of the trees.
In my stomach is a boiling flood
But the scent of grass, it cools my blood.
I crouch on my heels and begin to fumble
Stand up to greet another stumble.
Fear is rising in my chest
I step forward and hope for the best.
To my relief I don't fall
In fact I step on nothing at all.
There is a thundering in my ears
The foamy spray confirms my fears.
The waterfall comes up to meet me,
The milky drops fly high to greet me.
The thundering becomes a wail,
My arms and legs begin to flail,
Can't see,
Can't hear,
Can't breathe,
Think I'm dying,
Then I am flying.

Rachael O'Hanlon (12)
Torquay Grammar School for Girls, Torquay

If I Could Turn Back Time

If I could turn back time I would not do that thing
I would not do that thing I did to her
She was only small, not old enough to handle what I did to her
My very own sister, my own flesh and blood!

My sister was great, achieving at everything
I was so proud at first - as long as she was not better than me
But as we grew, you would have been blind not to see
That I, the older jealous, spiteful sister
I could not handle the amazingness of her
So I was hard and cruel, not the loving sister I was told to be.

I broke her down, bit by bit
Picking away at that old sacred sister bond we used to share
No longer any midnight feasts, of telling secrets and giggling all night
There was too much tension, so much hate weighing on my shoulders
I emotionally killed her dead inside
I stabbed her heart, cracked her skull.

But I love my sister, don't' get me wrong
I know now that it was not her
It was me, the older, jealous, spiteful sister
If I could turn back time I would not do that thing
I would not do that thing I did to her.

Annabel Seymour (14)
Torquay Grammar School for Girls, Torquay

Just Dreaming

I have come to the borders of sleep
No turning back - it's too late
Caressing cold darkness too deep
I am safe, I don't want to wake

No turning back - it's too late
No secrets, no lies to tell
I am safe, I don't want to wake
I am under the dreamtime spell

No secrets, no lies to tell
Nothing is what it seems
I am under the dreamtime spell
I float in the shadows of dreams

Nothing is what it seems
Caressing cold darkness too deep
I float in the shadows of dreams
I have come to the borders of sleep.

Emily Heathcote (13)
Torquay Grammar School for Girls, Torquay

When A Flower Dies

Who looks up when a flower dies
And still amongst the grasses lies,
When petals fall without a sound
Trodden to the cold stone ground,
Bright colours fade to stony grey
And once-sweet scents now fade away,
When just as all living things must
One more small beauty turns to dust,
And, wrapped up in their own affairs
No one sees and no one cares?

Rose Brennan (15)
Torquay Grammar School for Girls, Torquay

Lights Out

Midnight is the form of darkness
An empty space filled with the sorrow of the world
A curtain of black velvet outlining the sky
Midnight is lights out

Gangsters are the form of violence
Brutally hurting the souls of the Earth
Tough humans attacking innocent people
Gangsters turn the lights out

Bedtime is the form of peace
A time of relaxation and silence
Drifting in and out of life
Bedtime turns the light out

Lights out is the form of the world
Completely turning off everything
We all have a light to turn off
Yet there will always be one on somewhere.

Hannah Smith (13)
Torquay Grammar School for Girls, Torquay

The Sea

The stormy sea
Whistling, howling, gushing
The waves like massive scary monsters
About to gobble you up
The sky like a pit of darkness
It makes me feel terrified
The sea is a roaring lion
But suddenly as quiet as a cat sleeping
Peaceful, calm, soft
Like a gentle hand has soothed it
The sea
Just like the ups and downs of life.

Chloe Tomkinson (11)
Torquay Grammar School for Girls, Torquay

Suicidal Murder

The hands of the clock are still
Frozen in time and the night's cold chill
Out of the shadows she emerges, pale
And reaches for the now unmoving scale
Long fingers push the hands the other way
Trying to turn back time, one hundred days
For it is a year ago now she committed the crime,
A knife in the back, a slit, a red line,
She wishes now she had not been so hasty
They caught her red-handed, her face pale and pasty
She was found guilty in her trial and sentenced
Murder, life, never to see the sun again
They imprisoned her weeping in cold, merciless chains,
Forever to dream of freedom, no pain,
But it would finish now, alone in a cell,
She rips the sheet to a rope and knots it well
Around her neck the short loop hangs
Tight as a vice, sharp as a fang.
A short jump and it is done
The breath is stolen from her young, healthy lungs
As darkness clouds in all she can think as she dangles her feet
Are these four words, murderer, liar, vengeance, deceit.

Georgina McLennan (13)
Torquay Grammar School for Girls, Torquay

Memories

Memory is an important part of life.
Memory is always there to help to remember things, important
          things of life.
Memories are always a reminder of the important features
        of people's families.

Memories are short.
Memories are long.
Memories of happiness
Because they are fun.

Memories are short.
Memories are long.
Memories make you cry.
Because they are a reminder of everything.

Memories.
History.
Days gone by.
Special events.
Happy thoughts.
Sad thoughts.
How many more to come?

Courtney Giles-Buchanan (12)
Torquay Grammar School for Girls, Torquay

If Only

If you could have just one wish
Then what would your wish be?
A wish sure to come true
Think and then you'll see

Would you wish for the gleaming sun
To shine all year round
Or would you wish to fly away
And never touch the ground?

If you could live just one day
As somebody new
Who would you swap places with
Or would you stay as you?

Would you choose a pop star
And live a day like them
Or would you choose to stay yourself
Cos you're happy without them?

If you could ask just one question
That would be answered at last
Any question that you like
For future, present or past.

Would you ask of the planets
What's it like out there
To float around in space all day
Without a single care?

Your answers may be entirely different
But what counts is that they're yours
There is no right or wrong response
Nor any rules or laws.

Jennifer Huntington (13)
Torquay Grammar School for Girls, Torquay

Why Me?

Shuffling through the school gates
People staring, singling me out
I am the bottom of the pack,
Looked down on by the rest of the world.
Why me?

Pursued in the corridors
Thrown up against a wall,
Threatened, my pride bleeding
Droplets of my soul.
Why me?

Standing, shaking in the bathroom,
Salty tears squeezing from my eyes,
Others pass, notice me but walk away.
It's not their problem.
Why me?

Names shouted across the playground,
People want to help but think
Why should they when no one else will?
Lowering my eyes to the floor in shame.
Why me?

Lunch money taken, my possessions torn,
Strewn across the floor like fragments of my childhood.
Could you really call something that has caused me so much pain

a life?

Why me?

But today will be my day.
Today I will triumph.
Once I reach the ground far below
There will be no more pain.
It won't be me anymore.

Beth Dyer (13)
Torquay Grammar School for Girls, Torquay

I Wish

I wish I lived in a fairy tale
Where there were no thunderstorms or a strong gale
I wish I lived in castles
Unwrapping all my special parcels.
I wish I lived below the waves
Exploring all the underwater caves.

I wish I was a soaring bird
Flying, flying, not saying a word.
I wish I was a polar bear,
With all my soft, fuzzy hair.
I wish I was a galloping horse
Jumping over the jumping course.

I wish I had the world in my hands,
I'd clear up all those dirty cans.
I wish I had lots of money,
I'd spend it all, that would be funny.
I wish I had a very big house
But that would be as quiet as a mouse.

I wish for a lot of things
But let's see what the future brings!

Emily Harte (12)
Torquay Grammar School for Girls, Torquay

Nightmare

I have come to the borders of sleep
The unforgiving land
Where all thought is lost
Is drained
Where there is no escape.

Darkness swamps me with fear
All life disappears
A mystery unsolved
An unknown land to discover
And all the time in the world.

All ambition becomes forgotten
And all hope drifts away
The light at the end of the tunnel
Switches off
I feel immune to the world.

Misery is how I feel
Misery with no ending
Taking over my dreams
Then misery stops
I wake up.

Amy Woolfenden (12)
Torquay Grammar School for Girls, Torquay

The Flea

As I walked across the rocks one day
I saw a gull across the bay.
Perched on that gull there was a flea,
And this is what it said to me.

'I do not want to live no more!
Life on this gull is quite a bore,
And the sea wind gives a terrible roar,
I do not want to live no more!'

My jaw dropped down in surprise
This flea was not being very wise!
So I sat him down and calmly said,
'Mr Flea there is something wrong with your head!

You should want to live much, much more!
Life on this gull may be a bore
And the sea wind may give a terrible roar
But you should want to live much, much more!'

He looked at me with his beady eyes
And then he gave a sorrowful sigh.
'I have only one dream, it starts when
I join the circus and then, oh then

I would want to live life much more
My life would not at all be a bore!
The crowds cheering would be the only roar,
I would want to live my life much more!'

And so he skipped across the sand
With a tiny top hat and coat in hand.
And joined the circus with much glee
To become the best lion tamer in the whole of Fiji!

Kathryn McGhee (14)
Torquay Grammar School for Girls, Torquay

The Bubble

Every day is the same
You get up; you go to school to feel the same pain.
You look around corners to see if it's safe.
You avoid quiet places
You stay near familiar faces.
You go the long way to school
Your number one rule.
But you and they know you can't hide forever.
Eventually it happens on a cold winter's day,
There's nowhere to hide and no one to stand in their way.
Taunting, cursing, hurting,
Always the same.
You think of a happy place,
With fluffy clouds and butterflies.
You imagine you're in a bubble
So when they hit you
You pretend there is no pain.
Then it stops with one last kick
No tears, just fears.
You can't tell anyone,
Not your mum, sister or your teacher.
You keep it to yourself
Yourself and your bubble
No matter how many kicks and hits
You will never tell a soul
You'll just curl up in a ball
And think I'll just let it be.

Melissa King (14)
Torquay Grammar School for Girls, Torquay

Autumn

Autumn is the crisp brown leaves which dance upon the wind.
Autumn is the morning dew which scatters the plains with jewels.
Autumn is the morning sun which casts nets of light.
Autumn is the robin red who begins to show his face.

Autumn is the rough wind blowing on your face.
Autumn is the soft cashmere of the silken scarf.
Autumn is the rain falling from the covered grey sky.
Autumn is the dry texture of the burgundy leaves.

Autumn is the coloured leaves which crunch under wellington boots.
Autumn is the birdsong call chirped throughout the land.
Autumn is the laughing of children wrapped up all warm and sung.
Autumn is the howling gale ringing in our ears.

Autumn is the scent of pine cones all along the ground.
Autumn is the lingering of damp creeping from the shadows.
Autumn is the waft of smoke from the roaring fire.
Autumn is the smell of wheat carrying on the wind.

Autumn is the cold of the breeze filling our giant lungs.
Autumn is the fruits of harvest tickling at your taste buds.
Autumn is the swallowed hot chocolate filling our bodies with warmth.
Autumn is the melting frost like ice cubes tasting of cold.

Jennifer Grant (12)
Torquay Grammar School for Girls, Torquay

Writer's Block

This blank page is teasing me,
A white sheet of emptiness,
My mind, as vacant as the paper,
It's causing nothing but distress.

I sit here with my pen in hand
And suddenly, I have an idea,
I'll tell about my writer's block,
Now everything's becoming clear.

Slowly, as my mind wakes up,
The words begin to unfold,
My writer's block has disappeared,
My poem's about to be told.

For now, I have no control of my pen,
As the words tumble to the page,
My creativity starts to flow,
My mind begins to engage.

The more I write, the more I realise,
I have a way with words,
Until suddenly, all at once,
Away go all the words.

Abbie Bennett (13)
Torquay Grammar School for Girls, Torquay

Seasons

Winter is a carpet of thick snow falling faster and faster,
Winter is the young frost, twinkling in the morning sunlight,
Winter is daylight turning to darkness in the blink of an eye,
Winter is snowflakes coming.

Spring is the yellow daffodils waiting to be picked,
Spring is the fields growing fresh green grass,
Spring is glass raindrops melting on the newborn leaves,
Spring is a new beginning.

Summer is the warm sun spreading a layer of happiness,
Summer is green tomatoes slowly turning red,
Summer is fields coated in ten-foot sunflowers,
Summer is the sweltering heat.

Autumn is a rainbow of colours coating the dry morning leaves,
Autumn is red, yellow, orange all around us,
Autumn is a cool breeze fanning my face,
Autumn is leaves falling.

Ellie Aitchison (12)
Torquay Grammar School for Girls, Torquay

Spring

Spring is animals being born,
Spring is fields flourishing with corn,
Spring is flowers coming into bloom,
Spring is a lazy afternoon.

Spring is clouds that leisurely drift by,
Spring is kites that always fly,
Spring is blossom turning to flower,
Spring is colour to devour.

Spring is a breath of fresh air,
Spring is something that I love to share,
Spring is something young and new,
Spring is something pure and true.

Spring is grass turning a thriving green,
Spring is a sight that must be seen,
Spring is the sweet song of birds,
Spring is something to describe with words.

Jessica Bourne (13)
Torquay Grammar School for Girls, Torquay

I Loved The Way . . .

I loved the way we wished
We were fish and swam in the sea,
I loved the way I could talk to you
The way I could tell you anything.

I loved the way we wished we were kites
Flying through the sky,
I loved the way we had so much fun
Like the day could just go on.

I loved the way we wished we were bees
So we could see everything,
I loved the way I could just be me
And not pretend to be like someone else.

You and me together always
Against the world,
Wishes do come true
But I'm just happy to be me!

Meg Hackley (12)
Torquay Grammar School for Girls, Torquay

Wild Horses

Way up on the plains
Wild horses toss their manes
Watching foals at their sides
A creature waits and hides
Two foals went wandering away
One a chestnut, the other a bay.
When the time was right
The creature leapt with all its might
Landing on one of the pair,
The creature knows it has not a second to spare.
But with a mighty snort
The creature knew it was caught
As the stallion lashed out
The creature was thrown about.
With one last stare,
It ran as a hare
Drawing himself up to full height
The stallion reared as he had won the fight!

Jessica Powell (12)
Torquay Grammar School for Girls, Torquay

Fly Away

A peasant walks along The Strand
A feather in her hand,
She longs to roam and fly away
But how she cannot say.

She cannot see, she cannot see
And yet this small thought pleases me,
To truly know in my half heart
That she is happy in the part.

A peasant walks along The Strand
A feather in her hand,
She longs to roam and fly away
But how she cannot say.

She has no job, she has no fee
But still she lives so happily,
She thinks her thoughts of a child
Trapped in the body of forty-nine.

A peasant walks along The Strand
A feather in her hand,
She longs to roam and fly away
But how she cannot say.

A man walks and takes her palm
They're linked to keep her calm,
But instead of making her feel best
He stabs her in the chest.

A peasant lies along The Strand
They all saw her live her pain,
Yet no one will proclaim
Why won't anyone proclaim?

Catherine Seymour (12)
Torquay Grammar School for Girls, Torquay

What Does Winter Bring?

What does winter bring
Apart from coldness, wind and rain?
The long torturing nights
Will we see light again?

For people who are homeless,
For people who are lost,
What will the night do to them
And at what cost?

It could give them all an illness
Or make them feel pain,
They could lose all of their hope that night
Will they see light again?

What about the lonely
Are they at any risk?
They have no one to turn to
Will they get through the mist?

What does winter bring to us
The rich fortunate few?
Thick clothes, warming fires and Christmas time
There's no hardship for you.

How often is it every year
When we think about cold people outside?
They're suffering and need help, but do we care
When we're snug and warm inside?

So when it's winter this year
And the hard times come again
We should share our happy Christmas
Protect the needy from the pain.

Eve Ryan (12)
Torquay Grammar School for Girls, Torquay

Dream World

Enter the world beyond belief,
Where imagination flows free,
Fountains of gold and silver
And tales of adventure roam.

Dragons soar in the amber skies
While sirens sing their entrancing song,
Humans creep around the lush forests,
As the harpies let out a piercing screech.

Grass rustles as a chimera dashes past
Hunting its prey as a cat would a mouse
Silently stalking the unsuspecting victim
Ready to pounce at any given moment.

The quiet forest fills with a deathly scream
As the chimera catches its helpless prey,
Birds flock around the enormous kill
Waiting for the chimera to leave.

The amber sunset changes to a black void
As the cyan moon rises into the dark sky
Everything becomes foggy and dim
As you wake from this eerie dream.

Gabriela Voelske (12)
Torquay Grammar School for Girls, Torquay

Spring Is On The Way

Flowers burst open
And share your bloom.
Daffodils blow your trumpets
Let people know spring is here.
Bluebells ring aloud,
Spread the message
Spring is on the way!

Bunnies trim the grass,
Fill people with pleasure.
Lambs bleat your hearts out
Say goodbye to winter.
Foals stumble and leap,
Spread the message
Spring is on the way!

Sunshine make the days longer
Warm my heart.
Clouds blow away
Disperse into nothingness.
Rain don't ruin spring,
Just go away
Spring is on the way!

Rebecca Cronin (11)
Torquay Grammar School for Girls, Torquay

Will You Remember?

Will you remember
Me when I've gone
Far away from you?

Will you remember
The times that we've had
Strolling on moonlight sands
The good things and bad
The laughs and the tears?

Will you remember
The moments we've shared
The sunsets we've watched
The times we have dared
Jumping off skyscrapers backwards?

Will you remember
The places we've been?
Blackpool, Barmouth, Birmingham?
The wonder we've seen
Seals breaking through waves.

Will you remember
The times we've had
The good things and bad
The moments we've shared
The times we've dared
The places we've been
The wonders we've seen
And
Will you remember
Me?

Sarah Wiseman (12)
Torquay Grammar School for Girls, Torquay

Never Any Use

I am old and wretched
Trying to get back to my body,
But it is no use
Never any use, never.

I am lonely for evermore
I try for centuries
Or that is what it feels like
Never any use, never.

Sometimes I feel I've done it
But in the end I turn out wrong.
I've been in nearly everyone's body,
But not my own.

I am a spirit, a long-lost spirit,
How I try and try and try!
But my owner doesn't like me,
Never any use, never.

I can't die,
Although I wish I could.
But then my body would die too
Never any use, never.

I fly around making noises,
Trying to stun my owner,
So I can get back in.
Never any use, never.

But now I've done it,
I want to escape again,
I want to be free,
So it's back to the beginning for me.

Emma Pottle (12)
Torquay Grammar School for Girls, Torquay

Dreaming

D is for dreams that haunt your nights
  the ghostly shapes that give you frights.
R for remembering the dreams we've had
  whether they're good or whether they're bad
E is for echoes of memories past
  of happier times you wished would last.
A for amazing fantasy times
  of wild worlds and silent mimes.
M for monsters under the stairs
  growling and snarling hiding in lairs.
I for illusions of magical things
  flying away with fairy wings.
N for nightmares, sadness and grief
  that makes us need a handkerchief.
G for goodnight as we go up to bed
  no bad dreams here, there's good ones ahead.

Katie Needham (12)
Torquay Grammar School for Girls, Torquay

Spiders

Spiders here and spiders there

S mall as a pea
P esky to me
I n and out
D ash about
E ager to scare
R un out his lair!

Spiders here and spiders there.

Rachel Norman (11)
Torquay Grammar School for Girls, Torquay

The Photograph

A girl standing knee-deep in snow, her eyes are smiling,
> shiny and brown.
Her chubby face shows all the happiness in her heart.
A pile of snow with eyes, a mouth and a sunny yellow hat perched
> on its head
A carrot nose and twiggy arms that look as though
They could snap at any moment from the weight of the snow.
Behind her are snow-topped trees, perfect and glistening
> as if from a fairy story.
More fluffy white drops of snow settle on the ground like a blanket
> knitting itself.
The sky is metallic grey, it seems as though you could reach out
> and touch it.
Her pale white face looks numb
Although she doesn't show any sign of cold or pain; just happiness.

Lucy Kember (11)
Torquay Grammar School for Girls, Torquay

Mystery?

M is for memories that haunt you back
> they remind you of horrible things that you lack.
Y is for yonder, far, far away,
> where you are trapped you might have to stay.
S is for scary, it's really bad,
> it's spooky and dark and creepy and sad.
T is for terrible ghosts and ghouls,
> they're almost as bad as going to school.
E is for everlasting nightmares and dreams,
> filled with monsters and spooky themes.
R is for running away from your fears,
> when you find them near you burst into tears.
Y is for you to find the key,
> to unlock the answer to this mystery!

Emma Hardy (11)
Torquay Grammar School for Girls, Torquay

The Wind

The wind can take you places
Here, there and everywhere.
Pack your bags and suitcases
Because the wind can take you places.

You may go on your travels
Up and down, round and round.
And side to side, back and forward
Because the wind can take you places.

The wind can take you places
Here, there and everywhere.
Pack your bags and suitcases
Because the wind can take you places.

You may be here on your travels
African tribes drumming.
America's bands blowing their trumpets
Because the wind can take you places.

The wind can take you places
Here, there and everywhere.
Pack your bags and suitcases
Because the wind can take you places.

You may see on your travels
From Sydney Bridge to Eiffel Tower.
From every corner to every flower
Because the wind can take you places.

The wind can take you places
Here, there and everywhere.
Pack your bags and suitcases
Because the wind can take you places.

Annabel Strickland (12)
Torquay Grammar School for Girls, Torquay

I Remember

I remember a time
When people were happy
Without scary machines
Do you?

I remember a time
When there was no war
Only peace
Do you?

I remember a time
When people walked
Instead of polluting the world with cars
Do you?

I remember a time
When music was real
Instead of computer-generated sounds
Do you?

I remember a time
When the dodo existed
Before the humans killed them
Do you?

I don't remember a time
When this poem made any sense
To anyone but me
Do you?

Denice Chung (11)
Torquay Grammar School for Girls, Torquay

Ice-Skating

I step out
Onto the slippy ice
Staring at
My ruby-red skates.

I wobble,
I jerk slowly clinging
On the bars
Looking at crisp ice.

So worried,
Standing on vicious ice,
Suddenly,
No worries at all.

I am free,
Fast and flowing, whoosh,
Exciting,
To be on hard ice.

Warm, knotted,
Scarf wrapped right round and round,
Sharp ice skates
Crystal-white laces.

Midnight-black,
Padded coat right on me,
Whipping so,
Behind with a speed.

Whee, whoosh, whea!
Dodging loads of people,
Taking speed,
I'm dazzled by fun.

I am free,
Fast and flowing, whoosh,
Exciting,
To be on hard ice.

Lucy Wheeler (11)
Torquay Grammar School for Girls, Torquay

They Just Don't Think!

People on boats have so much fun
They lazily guzzle food and beer
And laugh as they throw bottles overboard
They just don't think!

People barbecue on the beach
Munching happily on their burgers
Then leave deadly metal in the sand
They just don't think!

Fishermen chug off out to sea
And catch shimmering shoals of fish
But they carelessly lose hooks and nets
They just don't think!

Then beaches are ruined, no longer safe,
Turtles choking on plastic bags.
Seabirds pierced with wicked hooks,
Dolphins coiled and drowned in nets.
Oh, how I wish they would think.

Ellie Lewis (11)
Wareham Middle School, Wareham

Dogs

All different breeds and all different kinds
Small and big, long and wide
Come in all sorts of colours from white, tan and black
Pointy ears, floppy ears, curly and straight.

But when they are young their teeth are like needles
Just be careful or they will have your ankles
Just make sure your shoes are put in the cupboard
Or you may just find one in a hole down the garden.

Likes chasing balls and fetching sticks
Never gets tired, always ready for a trick
Loves playing with dogs and chasing cats
A four-legged friend who's one of a kind.

Rachel Taylor (11)
Wareham Middle School, Wareham

Ten Baby Dragons

Ten baby dragons
Flying in a line
One flew into an aeroplane
Then there were nine.

Nine baby dragons
Having fun at the fête
One fell off the roller coaster
Then there were eight.

Eight baby dragons
Trying to fly to Heaven
One met a nasty devil
Then there were seven.

Seven baby dragons
In a nasty fix
One was chased by a grumpy seagull
Then there were six.

Six baby dragons
Practising how to dive
One missed the diving board
So now there are five

Five baby dragons
Forced to do some chores
One was attacked by the washing machine
Then there were four.

Four baby dragons
Fighting a monster bee
One got stung on the tummy
So then there were three.

Three baby dragons
Locked in the loo
One got flushed down the toilet
So now there are two.

Two baby dragons
Eating chocolate buns
Sadly one was poisoned
So now there's only one.

One baby dragon
Sad he's the only one
So he flew into space
So now there's none.

Harry Fagan (11)
Wareham Middle School, Wareham

What Bad Day?

Grrr, time to get up
It's only six-thirty
And what on earth is in my cup?
Downstairs is the same
Taz dog goes mad biting and jumping
Mathew is shouting but my head is thumping
Off to school bus
It's raining and cold
Coughing and sneezing
Oh where is the bus? It's freezing
School is no better
Just can't read a letter
Lunch at last but not so fast
Pickle and cheese
Oh but please
Matthew's lunch I will not munch
Oh no, I've missed the bus
Now Mum will make a fuss.
A face like thunder
A mood to match
I get in the back
And don't make a sound
At last home safe and sound
My evening is more quiet
No disasters
Friday the thirteenth is over tomorrow
Soon to come.

Lauren Davis (11)
Wareham Middle School, Wareham

The Sea

The sea is a long blue carpet
It is a far-off blue horizon
It is an angry bull belting rocks
In the deep ocean

The sea is a playground for boats
It is a heaven for kayaks
It is pool of happiness
For all things

But the sea is a dumping ground
A place for rubbish and oil
We throw waste in the sea
And it is bad

This is our time we can change these things
Helping the sea will do us all good
It will let us keep on doing the things we like
Like water sports and other water activities

If we can keep the sea unpolluted
We will have a great time.

Tom Watts (11)
Wareham Middle School, Wareham

Logs

I chopped a lot of logs today
We had to they were in the way
We chopped and chopped till we were sore
And then we chopped and chopped some more.
We moved them in the wheelbarrow
Down our alleyway which is narrow
Some fell out along the way
We'll pick them up another day.
We stacked them up in our log shed
And then we put ourselves to bed.

Robert Evans (11)
Wareham Middle School, Wareham

My Family Poem

M y family is funny but sometimes very weird
Y oung Daniel is fascinated with the seventies wigs

F oreign my cousins may be but also English
A nd I still know what they say to me
M y mum is very funny, kind and
 I s very useful to get to school
L ovely Thomas is very sweet
Y ou should see him walking around, smiling and laughing

P arents and family are the best thing to have
O f all so make use of them and have fun
E ating, playing and
M aking your life worthwhile.

Lauren Chevalier (11)
Wareham Middle School, Wareham

Snooze Fest

I'm bored
There's nothing to do
Only boring homework
Sleeping is more exciting
At this very moment
I'd much rather be outside
Playing football with my mates,
Riding my bike
Anything rather than doing my homework
On a scorching hot day like this.
Oh look at that, I've done my homework
Now this snooze fest is over
And so is my moaning!

Tom Lavin (11)
Wareham Middle School, Wareham

Forest

Forest fans scream
The atmosphere is so extreme
Fans dramatically sing a song
The crowd starts to sing along
The team appear from the tunnel
The referee blows his jet-black whistle
He tosses a coin, 'Heads or tails?'
The nervous team inhales and exhales
The ball flies through the air
The referee is so unfair
Fans tensely watch the game
Forest striker takes an aim
The ball whizzes past the keeper
Nottingham Forest are really super!

Molly Tighe (11)
Wareham Middle School, Wareham

The Roman Army

The Roman Legion Army
Marching all day long
Killing people they don't like
They really must be barmy.

The Roman Legion troop
Fighting all day long
Taking over people's land
And signing donkaty doop!

The Roman Legion people
Walking up the hillside
Throwing all their sprees
And eating up all the trifle!

Tim Harrison (11)
Wareham Middle School, Wareham

Yu-Gi-Oh Cards

My Yu-gi-oh cards
Swap 'em, trade 'em, Yu-gi-oh
Yu-gi-oh cards, cool.

Monsters, spells and traps
Maybe a magic card too
My Yu-gi-oh cards.

The rules say life points
Face down, face up, activate
Attack, defend friends.

Weakest and strongest
The shadow game we will play
Bow to the shadows.

You are banished
Be gone to the shadow realm
The chaos is end.

Marc Grenville-Cleave (11)
Wareham Middle School, Wareham

A Spiral

Oh how fun it would be to slide down a spiral.
We would go down together, you and me.
How fun it would be to go so fast,
To zoom down a spiral.
We would never want to stop as time went past.
How fun it would be to dance and tango down a spiral.
So when we went past others they would glance.
How fun it would be to scream and shout down a spiral.
But sadly all of this was a happy dream,
So now the dream ends,
So go tell your friends.

Rose Legg (11)
Wareham Middle School, Wareham

Ten Warty Witches

Ten warty witches
Went into a stone mine
One fell unconscious
So then there were nine.

Nine warty witches
Went to a school fête
One went to see the headmaster
So then there were eight.

Eight warty witches
Tried vodka watermelon
One got drunk
So then there were seven.

Seven warty witches
Went collecting sticks
One ran away
So then there were six.

Six warty witches
Went to see Uncle Clive
One got arrested
So then there were five.

Five warty witches
Tried to catch a boar
One got stabbed
So then there were four.

Four warty witches
Went for a swim in the sea
One froze to death
So then there were three.

Three warty witches
Went to the zoo
One got put in a cage
So then there were two.

Two warty witches
At a theme park having fun
One fell out of the roller coaster
So then there was one.

One warty witch
Not having fun
She grabbed herself a dagger
So then there were none.

Alex Lane (11)
Wareham Middle School, Wareham

Can I Have A Puppy?

Please Mum,
Please Mum,
Please, please, please.

Please Mum,
Please Mum,
Please, please, please.

I'll feed him,
I'll walk him,
I swear I'll even talk to him.

I'll play every day
And he'll never run away.

Please Pappy,
You love to make me happy.

I'll pick up after him
And he really won't eat from the bin
I'm honest and true,
I'll let him out when he needs to.

Please Dad,
Please Dad,
Please, please, please.

Please Dad,
Please Dad,
Please, please, please.

Theresa Cullinane (12)
Wareham Middle School, Wareham

The Race

The race car driver races the tracks,
Racing at super top speeds to reach the max.
He tries to win races and will never give up,
His hopes and dreams are to win the cup.

He trains all day and all night,
From sun to moon, the finish is in sight.
But will be win? No one knows.
The racer's dreams have suddenly froze.

The engines roar, the pistols fire,
The race begins, the smell of burning tyre.
Third place, second place, the head to head,
He needs full throttle to get ahead.

Suddenly the finish is in sight,
His engine roaring like dynamite.
Just one more straight, then the race is up.
And yes, finally, he wins the cup.

Ryan Cole (11)
Wareham Middle School, Wareham

Dog

My dog is very active
My dog is very fun
Her long golden fluffy tail
And her excellent sense of smell
Her walks are always long
She knows the way and can't go wrong
Blue and purple flowers
She would run for hours and hours!

Louisa Crabb (12)
Wareham Middle School, Wareham

Seasons Greetings!

Spring is full of flowers
Summer is full of sun
Autumn is full of leaves
Winter is full of *snow*.

Spring is warm
Summer is hot
Autumn is cold
Winter is bleak.

Spring is fit for skipping
Summer is fit for swimming
Autumn is fit for leaf fights
Winter gives you frost bites.

Spring has long been gone
Summer is basically over!
Autumn's on its way
But winter's two seasons away!

Louise Bennett (12)
Writhlington School, Writhlington

The Thing That Makes A Noise

It screams
and beams
as it sits in its chair.

It bangs
and clangs
as it hangs on people's hair.

It struggles
and bubbles
as it goes to bed.
What could it be?
It's a baby you see.

Dannielle Pearce (11)
Writhlington School, Writhlington

The Worst Day Of My Life

The worst day of my life,
Was when Mum came home
And told me she had cancer
And she needed an operation.

I didn't know what to say,
Inside I felt so sad and lonely,
But I knew that she would be alright,
She's my mum and she can't leave me.

The day after the operation,
Dad took us into the hospital to see Mum,
I was so pleased that she was still alive,
I thought I would never see her again.

A couple of days later,
Mummy came home,
But we knew the fight wasn't over,
She still needed after treatment.

Three years later,
We had more bad news,
The cancer had spread,
In bones in her hips.

So here we are now,
Of round two of the cancer,
I thought it was over,
How wrong can you be?

Katie Beck (12)
Writhlington School, Writhlington

Space

Comets shooting through space, *swoosh,*
Stars shimmering brightly, *twinkle,*
Planets orbiting the sun, *zoom,*
Universes being made, *boom,*
What will be next to enter the void?

Sam Maggs (12)
Writhlington School, Writhlington

Hawk

Scanning the ground for the tasty morsel it desires,
Locking on to the juicy creature
It swoops down for what seems like the first meal in a week;
Silently, it gets closer, closer . . .

Snap!

Slowly,
It gobbles the creature
Down
Letting the flavours wander across its tongue;
It is filled with the sensation of being full again.

Its sensitive ears hearing the sound of a thing . . .

As fast as a falling brick it is back on its branch,
Surveying the noise-maker wandering by on its four round feet.
As soon as the hawk is sure it is gone
It circles again looking for its next meal,
Round and round
Rising slowly on the air shaft,
Regaining height
To continue for the never-ending hunger to subside.

Samuel Hopkins (12)
Writhlington School, Writhlington

Sand

The long grains of it
On the beach, *shh!*
The children playing with it,
Get your buckets, *shh!*
The sand in the wind blows
In the sea with all the creatures, *ssh!*
The sand!
The sand!

Nubia Abaka (12)
Writhlington School, Writhlington

Life

Life is like a journey,
It can take you wherever you want,
You can write your life story in any size font.
As you pick and choose your life career,
Try not to make too many mistakes,
Don't take a lot of breaks,
You only live once.
Every time you walk down the street you meet something new,
If you meet someone and think eew,
Don't judge a book by its cover,
Think of all the people in the world that can't make their
dreams come true.
You can, yes you,
Never give up on your dreams
Because you *only live once,* remember that!

Zoe Fear (12)
Writhlington School, Writhlington

The Twin Towers

Yes, I was there,
When the Twin Towers were hit bare.
I felt tragic inside,
But there was nowhere to hide.

All the people on the plane,
Their thoughts must have driven them insane.
Imagine how they must have felt,
Dying like this but they could not help.

Among the people that have died,
Many people wept and cried.
The Twin Towers are now in ashes,
That was made by all of the crashes.

Adam Simmons (12)
Writhlington School, Writhlington

Mr Loud

Mr Loud was my teacher,
He has a dog and a cat,
He loves to work at the school,
But has almost got the sack.

It was on a Friday you see,
The last day of the week,
He's louder on these Fridays,
And Miss Hoskin was having a peek.

She went from class to class,
As she was walking down the hall,
She heard screaming and shouting,
She thought someone had had a fall.

She looked in the door
And saw Mr Loud,
He was bawling and shouting,
He scared the whole crowd.

My friends and I,
Had our hands over our ears,
I think all this screaming,
Scared all my fears.

Sir had to go to the office,
So we got the lesson off,
I actually felt sorry for him,
Because he's such a big soft.

And that was my teacher,
Mr Loud he is,
He's not so loud these days,
But I remember him as this.

Katy Jane Larcombe (12)
Writhlington School, Writhlington

The Oracle

With a hiss and a crack, the lightning rolled,
Illuminating the sky,
The green smoke steamed through the gaps,
In the broken flagstone floor
And behind the smoke was she,
The Oracle.

Her hands twisted gnarly wood,
Her eyes deep staring holes,
Her skin like crumbling newspaper,
Her hair was a matted, tangled mane
And behind it all,
Her gift was there,
The Oracle.

Then he came slicing through the wood,
A dashing knight with angel eyes,
He strode through the smoke,
Rusted blade held high
And knelt before her,
The Oracle.

She smiled her broken, gap-toothed smile
And reached out with a bony claw,
He looked at her with his angel eyes,
Again she smiled her gap-toothed smile
And told him what was true,
He left in shock back through the wood,
For the truth was harsh,
The truth was cruel,
The truth was her,
The Oracle.

Eleanor Owen (12)
Writhlington School, Writhlington

Graveyard

The gate creaked open
Trees hung low
I was in a graveyard.

I looked around
Horror is what I saw
I was in a graveyard.

The lightning flashed
Rain poured down
I was in a graveyard.

Something screamed
I turned around
I was in a graveyard.

A skeleton reached
To grab my throat
I was in a graveyard.

I fought and struggled
To gain control
I was in a graveyard.

It pulled a knife
It stabbed . . .

I went into a graveyard
I went into a graveyard
I am in a grave.

George Beechener (11)
Writhlington School, Writhlington

My Cat

It was a sunny day,
The sun was dawning,
I was waking up to a beautiful morning,
What a beautiful day, I was going to get a cat.
And there it was in its wonderful cage,
Looking up at me with a pleading face
And then it came to me,
I knew it would be a perfect cat for the whole of the family.

In the car on the way back home,
I looked at its face
And what a smiley face,
And I knew I had made another cat happy.
The next morning and I woke up,
It was lying beside my bed with the same face,
The happy face,
The thankful face
And it made me proud that I had made another cat happy!

Kirsty Cotter (11)
Writhlington School, Writhlington

Hallowe'en

Tonight is Hallowe'en,
Move to the rhythm, move to the beat, get on down
You'd better pick up your feet!
The trees are swirling!
The wind is howling!
The ghouls and ghosts have come,
You'd better find your mum!
For tonight is *Hallowe'en,*
Hallowe'en!
Hallowe'en!

Jazuela Wall (11)
Writhlington School, Writhlington

What's A Fairy?

Is a fairy a small magical human with wings?
Or is it a bird?
Or a ghost?
Is it a cartoon figure with wings and a wand?
What is a real fairy?
Do fairies bark like dogs?
Do they jump or hop like frogs?
Do fairies miaow like cats?
Or do they screech like bats?
Do fairies go shopping?
Do they eat or drink?
Do they smile and think?
What are fairies?
So, what do you think?

Ellena Doswell (11)
Writhlington School, Writhlington

Forever And A Day

Tonight is a story of love
And two broken hearts set by one.
No one can see their pain,
They need each other but know it can never be.

Her heart is in pieces,
Shattered on the ground.
He tries to pick them up for her,
But nothing helps.

So tell your father
And we can run
Far away from here
And stay together

Forever and a day.

Seona Alexander (14)
Writhlington School, Writhlington

Naughty Cats

Climbing up the dirty drain,
A silly little cat would play,
The plonky little cat would say,
Miaow, miaow as he climbed up the drain,
Scraping around for something to eat,
Scrap, scrap, scrap after another,
He finds in those dirty drains.

He climbs back down to find . . .
Another cat fast asleep
Just beneath him
Waiting to eat
But secretively he climbs down
And gets away.

He feels guilty
So off he toddles back
With a stomp here and a screech there,
He finally makes it there,
That poor little cat still there asleep
Wakes up to find
Another cat looking over.

With a big jump the tiny little cat
Runs away,
So off with a faster run the other cat runs to find her,
When found
The poor cat is shaking,
So off the boy goes to find some food for her,
Squeezing through tight holes and tiny gaps he finds something,
Takes it back to the lady cat and lets her have it.

So she eats it and then isn't scared of the other cat,
The dirty little cats are found by a kind little boy
And are taken to his house to eat,
Drink and sleep,
In fact they never leave

So they feel amazing.

Tania Reason (12)
Writhlington School, Writhlington

The Spell

Her hair blew in the wind, black as coal,
Her face pale as a ghost, ready to scare you,
Her fingers were long and her nails like knives,
Ready to put a spell on you,
Her legs long and bendy, ready to sit on her broom,
The spell had been cast on her.

Running, running from the witch,
Through the wild wood,
Screaming, shouting for help,
Suddenly she was under the spell,
Nothing or no one could help her.

Blonde hair turning black,
Stubby fingers growing long,
Legs transforming into bendy ones,
Under the spell,
How could she go on?

She sat there on the floor,
She wept and wept,
The moon shone down,
It lifted her up in the air,
Swooping and diving.

Black hair turning blonde,
Long fingers shrinking back to small,
Bendy legs becoming stronger,
Free from the spell,
Her life could go on.

The tale of Rhiannon,
Is magical and mystical,
Strange and amusing,
No one would believe her tale,
Witches are real and moons are magic.

Aaliyah Porter (11)
Writhlington School, Writhlington

Teen Life

Why do you do that thing you do?
Can't you see it's harming you?
You take a puff and blow it out,
No one knows what you're all about.

Why do you do that thing you do?
Drinking alcohol just isn't you.
To you and your mates, it's all a laugh
But you could be reaching the end of your path.

Why do you do that thing you do?
Every weekend is just the same to you.
You sit around, getting high,
You're watching your life passing by.

Why do you do that thing you do?
A cut here, a slit there, blood all over you.
Even if your life's driving you mad,
Just stop and think, it can't be that bad.

How far would you go just to fit in?
Please be yourself – you can't fail to win.

Martha Cooper (14)
Writhlington School, Writhlington

Have You Ever . . . ?

Have you ever felt the morning sun
As it beams down when the day's just began?
Have you ever dreamt upon a midnight sky,
Wishing to soar with the stars so high?
Have you ever felt the warmth of a fire?
And when it leaves, there's a lasting desire.
Have you ever fallen amongst the sea?
A vast expanse surrounding me.
Have you ever been deeply in love?
Hearts entwined like fingers in a glove.
Have you ever felt the cold of death?
Everything encased for a final rest.

Joanne Clapp (14)
Writhlington School, Writhlington

Untitled

Standing still
All alone
Only the whisper of the wind
Watching
Children's laughter
Even when plural no sound.

Goalposts
Climbing frame
Years spent of fun
Generations
Smiling faces
Until tomorrow.

A man
Shimmering blade
Slow rhythmical chops
Picked up
In pieces
Lowered into the crusher

Everlasting silence.

(Tree)

Claire Andrade (14)
Writhlington School, Writhlington

Sweets

I looked up in the cupboard,
What did I see?
Little bags of sweeties staring at me,
Pity they were on the top shelf,
Not on the bottom,
Oh no, they will die and go rotten.
I lifted one leg up
Onto the drawer handle,
But fell into failure in a big bundle.

Billy Say (11)
Writhlington School, Writhlington

The Reason

Do you ever feel like you don't belong?
Have you ever felt alone?
Welcome to my world
And maybe if you opened your eyes you would see
This is me,
My life
So lonely
Until
I find it,
My reason for living,
The one thing in the world that makes me feel alive,
The fire growing bigger and brighter each day,
Taking over
Until
Nothing else seems right.

Caroline Rankin (14)
Writhlington School, Writhlington

The World

Why are we here in this world?
Are we just the guardians of this world?
Or are we the founders of the world?
Do we own our own world?
Or are we the enemies of this world?

We contaminate, litter and will eventually end this world,
We cannot stop it, end it or finish this world.
Millions live alone in the streets of our world,
No food, clothes or warmth. God what a world.
Help the world, or we won't know what the world will become . . .

Andrew Girvan (14)
Writhlington School, Writhlington

The Crow

Death messengers float across the plain
Scattering their dark feathery litter, like bad omens

Top-floor dwellers proudly watching
Over the sun-soaked land below

Little inky blotches boldly stand
Against the pastel evening glow

The spies of the skies roam around
Sleek in their sooty silky coats

Head down like working students,
Fishing through a sea of grass
For helpless, wriggling victims

They stream to base as the moon rises
From dusk to dawn they rest
And only occasional soft caws
Disturb the crowded community's peace.

Lauren Smith (14)
Writhlington School, Writhlington

Masks

I enter the room, but no one sees
All around vibrant colours whirl past
The music flows, flooding the chamber
Flickering lights fill the shadows.

Emotions are hidden behind masks
Glamorous eyes sparkle beneath patterns
Everyone is unique and pasts are unknown
I silently glide over to the refreshments.

Warm punch slides down my throat
Tasty bites are handed around
A man wanders over to me
Then we slide away to join the party.

Tabitha Eddleston (14)
Writhlington School, Writhlington

What We Take For Granted

Autumn's leaves swirl around
Raindrops splatter and tickle the window sill
Wind moves noiseless around the world
And gloomy clouds above them cry their sorrow
Trees whisper in morbid silence
Grass fades to squelching mud
And lives turn hard once again.

All day long they shiver in frostiness
Work in fields to tend to their crops
Wish of richness and education
Walk to and fro from the well
Seeking fresh water
At night they snuggle down to sleep
And rest for five hours or less.

Isn't there anything else for them
We get annoyed with the government for sending us to school
While they yearn for an education of any sort
Should we swap?
We hate our fresh fruit and vegetables
Milk and water
While they yearn for both
Should we swap our lives with them,
Or should we help them and start to be grateful?

Polly Eddleston (12)
Writhlington School, Writhlington

Sometimes

Sometimes I cry but there's no reason,
Sometimes I hurt myself for fun.
Sometimes I talk but no one listens
And end up staring at the sun.

Sometimes I look but don't see anything,
Sometimes I scream but no one hears.
My mask hides my hurt and feelings
I cannot hide from all my tears.

I need to open up and tell you,
All my thoughts, hopes and dreams.
People now are too stereotypical
In my Converse boots and skinny jeans.

I clench my fists and walk by slowly
Ignoring shouts, abuse and names.
I am who I am and cannot help it.
Why should I be the same?

As the black runs down from my eyes
I look at you and see inside.
I want to feel free and happy,
Stop trying and failing to hide.

Emma Shaw (14)
Writhlington School, Writhlington

World Of Words

Words make the world go round,
Round and round it goes,
Goes around and never stops,
Stops neither do words,
Words flow good and bad,
Bad and sad and all,
All the world can talk,
Talk in different ways,
Ways of speaking to one another,
Another tells how they feel,
Feel about each other,
Other shouldn't bottle it up,
Up tight inside,
Inside where fear can be,
Be from their happy side,
Side should tell,
Tell everyone,
Everyone should know,
Know then be so happy,
Happiness, not fear.

Jacqui Fee (14)
Writhlington School, Writhlington

A Fox

It has a lovely tail,
It rarely fails.

Its coat is shiny and red,
It hardly goes to bed.

It hunts for its food
And at this it's very good.

It has a pointy nose
And always does a pose.

It's a fox!

Alice Gouldbourne (12)
Writhlington School, Writhlington

Shall I Compare Thee?

'Shall I compare thee to a summer's day'?
 Well, why to a summer's day be compared?
 The scorching sun,
 The dreadful pollen in the air,
 The god-damned insects flying everywhere.
So, shall I compare thee to a spring day?
 Well, why to a spring day be compared?
 The spring showers,
 The urge to clean,
 The lambs to the slaughter, so small and lean.
So, shall I compare thee to a winter's day?
 Well, why to a winter's day be compared?
 The freezing wind,
 The violent chill,
 The frozen lakes, taking many a kill.
So, shall I compare thee to an autumn day?
 Well, why to an autumn day be compared?
 The call of migrating birds above,
 The dead leaves littering the ground,
 The annoying squirrels scuttering around.
So, what shall I compare to thee?
 Thou art beyond compare!

Guy Solomon (14)
Writhlington School, Writhlington

Heartbroken

As I walk away
My heart breaks.
I am alone,
Falling tears
Won't help me now.

Natasha Alsop (14)
Writhlington School, Writhlington

Bearded Dragon

Every day I wake up
I see
Sand
Branches
Rocks
And the outside world.

I like to eat
Locusts, crickets,
Salad and mealworms.
I like watching the people
Who look after me
Outside my cage,
Sometimes I go out,
I watch TV and sit on the pool table,
It's nice, but I get cold
And have to go back in my nice warm cage
Because the English climate is too cold.

In my cage
I usually sleep
Or eat
Or bask in the sun.
Sometimes I hide in my cave
Or burrow under the sand
Or climb high up on the branches.
I like my cage.

I am a bearded dragon
And that's how I'll stay
Until I die.

Emma Robertson (14)
Writhlington School, Writhlington

The Carousel

The carousel spins round
Taking me, taking you
Up and down
The horses go round and round
In a blue
Like a yo-yo at high speed.

It never stops
The lyrics just play on and on
Sending me dizzy
Messing with my head
All I see is the view
Flying past.

My heart's so cold
Because I just don't understand
Why time never stops
But everyone acts like it's going to
Right, right now
The end can't be that near.

The carousel spins round
Just won't stop
My heart beats
As time goes on
Like usual
But then . . .

Boom!

Helen Vipond (14)
Writhlington School, Writhlington

The Meaning Of Life

What is the meaning of life?
Is it to learn?
To learn about everything?
Or is it to turn,
All the directions in life?

What is the meaning of life?
Is it the happiness
From doing something new?
Or is it the sadness
From suffering too?

What is the meaning of life?
Is it to prevent animal extinctions
As the future nears?
Or is it to continue human generations,
In the later years?

Is there a meaning of life?
Or do we live life to
Discover the meaning?
No one knows the truth.

Kate Fawcett (14)
Writhlington School, Writhlington

Rolo

Rolo
My horse,
Fast as lightning,
Nickname Roly Mole,
Up and over the jumps,
Gliding, floating, flying through the air,
Down, down we're over jumps,
Cantering to the next,
Fast as lightning,
My horse
Rolo.

Bethan Lewis (11)
Writhlington School, Writhlington

Easter Is A . . .

Easter is a thousand colours, red and purple
Easter is a newborn baby lamb struggling to stand up
Easter is a sparrow darting to and fro
Easter is a thousand colours, purple and red.

Easter is a thousand colours, blue and yellow
Easter is a remembrance of Jesus' death
Easter is a holy holiday
Easter is a thousand colours, yellow and blue.

Easter is a thousand colours, orange and violet
Easter is a time of peace and rest
Easter is a sign of newborn baby animals
Easter is a thousand colours, violet and orange.

Joe Seymour (12)
Writhlington School, Writhlington

Washing Machine

Watch it swirl,
Watch it swish
In and out,
Round and round,
Swishy, swashy,
Squelch.

They go in dirty,
Swirl about,
Then they come out with a shout.
They come out clean
With a glean,
Swishy, swashy,
Squelch.

Rhiannon Batstone (12)
Writhlington School, Writhlington

My Brother

There he is, my brother Leon
On the grid, revving his engine,
His very own racing kart.

The gate goes up and off he goes.
The smell of fuel floats past me,
I run to the fence to watch.

Very slowly they head for the start line,
As the wheels turn faster and faster
The lights go green.

They fly past me, 60 miles per hour,
Someone comes spinning towards me
Phew, it wasn't Leon.

They're coming, Leon's fourth,
My dad starts running,
The red flag goes out.

Yet again, my brother's chance is gone,
Gone, gone, forever!
Well, until next time anyway.

Chloe Hilleard (11)
Writhlington School, Writhlington

Pollution

I can see it in the air,
Drifting slowly, flying high, swooping around,
Coming towards me.

I can see it in the stream,
Whistling loudly, howling, prowling around,
Coming towards me.

I can see it on the floor,
Gnashing, biting, fighting around,
Coming towards me.

It's angry and killing,
It's coming to get me.

I wake up, it's just a dream,
I am scared, alone,
I don't want to go outside,
I must hide, hide.

I can see into the future,
I can see where the world will end.

Maddie Norton Smith (12)
Writhlington School, Writhlington

Young Writers Information

We hope you have enjoyed reading this book - and that you will continue to enjoy it in the coming years.

If you like reading and writing poetry drop us a line, or give us a call, and we'll send you a free information pack.

Alternatively if you would like to order further copies of this book or any of our other titles, then please give us a call or log onto our website at www.youngwriters.co.uk

**Young Writers Information
Remus House
Coltsfoot Drive
Peterborough
PE2 9JX**

(01733) 890066